If I Were Satan

by

Dr. Kingsley Fletcher

All Scripture quotations are from
the Authorized King James Version of the Bible,
unless otherwise noted.

Dr. Kingsley Fletcher
P. O. Box 3070
Chapel Hill, NC 27515-3070

Destiny Image Publishers
P.O. Box 351
Shippensburg, PA 17257

ISBN 1-56043-034-6

For Worldwide Distribution
Printed in the United States of America

Finally, my brethren, be strong in the Lord, and in the power of his might. Put on the whole armour of God, that ye may be able to stand against the wiles of the devil. For we wrestle not against flesh and blood, but against principalities, against powers, against the rulers of the darkness of this world, against spiritual wickedness in high places. Wherefore take unto you the whole armour of God, that ye may be able to withstand in the evil day, and having done all, to stand. Stand therefore, having your loins girt about with truth, and having on the breastplate of righteousness; And your feet shod with the preparation of the gospel of peace; Above all, taking the shield of faith, wherewith ye shall be able to quench all the fiery darts of the wicked. And take the helmet of salvation, and the sword of the Spirit, which is the word of God:

Ephesians 6:10-17

Dedication

I dedicate this book:

To *the glory of the Lord*.

To *my wife, Martha*, who has been a tremendous strength to me in the ministry.

To all *those who need victory over Satan's works.*

Contents

Foreword

The devil is a hyper-religious, church-going, scripture-quoting fanatic. Does that statement surprise you? It shouldn't. Sometimes we Christians have a misconception about the enemy that causes us to think of his influence primarily in the areas of the "biggie" sins. We tend to forget that his warfare is particularly aimed at the people of God, and in order to touch them, his strategies must be subtle. Why do you think church folks are so prone to become involved in gossip, slander, backbiting, division, unforgiveness and bitterness? These are some of the devil's most effective weapons. If he can keep Christians fighting among themselves, he has rendered them ineffective.

Last year I celebrated my fiftieth year of public ministry. I may not know everything there is to know about the enemy, but I have learned some of his tactics over the years. There is one thing that I know about Satan that I like to tell other Christians: The Devil is God's devil. He is not a little god who rules and reigns apart from the purpose of God. The devil is a dog with a choke collar and God Almighty is holding the leash. Remember the opening chapter of the book of Job? Satan didn't barge in on God's heavenly staff meeting. He was required to be there!

Don't get me wrong. I'm not suggesting that the devil is powerless. What I am saying is that he is a liar, an accuser, a thief and a murderer. The power that he wields is stolen power. And, thank God, his days are numbered. Because of Jesus' perfect work on Calvary, the devil is a defeated foe.

I am delighted to have the privilege of recommending to you this book. Dr. Kingsley Fletcher is a young man whose experience far exceeds his years. ***If I Were Satan*** is a significant book in which he uncovers the tactics of the enemy. Many Christians who read this book will discover areas in which they have been deceived and thereby held captive. I sincerely believe that this book will be a means of setting many of God's people free from satanic influence.

After you have finished reading it, please don't store it on your bookshelf. Pass it on to a friend and allow the Holy Spirit to use it in their life also.

Bishop John L. Meares
Evangel Temple
Washington, D.C.

Introduction

I was born and raised in Africa, the so-called "jungle" or "dark continent." But I received the grace of God early in my life. Because of that, today I am experiencing His continuous blessings. I can say that I am not going under; I am going over. I am not defeated; I am victorious. I am not a loser; I am a winner. I will not dwell in darkness; I will rejoice in the light.

In the past, much of Africa has been given over to witchcraft, superstition and darkness. I thank God for delivering me from the power of the enemy. I found Christ as my Savior when I was only ten years old. Then, very early, God began to teach me about the enemy, about his tactics, and about the weapons which are available to us against him.

For more than twenty years now I have dedicated my life to tearing down the strongholds of Satan and building in their place the everlasting Kingdom of God.

It grieves me to see so many good people devastated by Satan's power in our modern world. It grieves me because it is not necessary, since health and healing, prosperity and blessing, salvation and everlasting life are available to us through Jesus Christ, God's Son.

Strangely enough, many people are afraid of God, yet they are not afraid of Satan. Many people do not respect the power of God, while they do respect the power of Satan. Many people are afraid to listen to God, but do listen to Satan. Many people are afraid to obey God, but they are willing to obey Satan.

This is all due to Satan's terrible ability to deceive. He is a master of deception, and our world is deceived by him. Good has become evil; and evil has become good. Right has become wrong; and wrong has become right.

In the pages of this book, I want to try to put myself in Satan's place and think as he thinks. Please don't misunderstand me and think that I am glorifying him in any way. I want to expose his lies in order to set the record straight.

My prayer is that the God of Abraham, Isaac and Jacob use the pages of this book to open YOUR eyes to the truth and deliver YOU from the snare of the fowler. May YOU find, through these pages, the freedom you have so desperately been seeking.

Dr. Kingsley Fletcher, Ph.D.
Chapel Hill, North Carolina

Part I

The Enemy and His Tactics

Chapter 1

A Real Enemy

Be sober, be vigilant; because your adversary the devil, as a roaring lion, walketh about, seeking whom he may devour: 1 Peter 5:8

Be self-controlled and alert. Your enemy the devil prowls around like a roaring lion looking for someone to devour. NIV

The reason God has commanded us to put on His armor is that we are facing a real enemy. We are in a real wrestling match. We are engaged in a real battle. Some believers already know it, but others still refuse to believe it. Whether you believe it or not doesn't change the truth.

You are in a battle. Somebody is plotting your defeat. Somebody is tracking you for the kill. Somebody is setting traps for you in the most unexpected places. Somebody is dedicated to fighting against you every hour of every day. He will not rest until he sees you fallen. He fully intends to kill you. He is determined to destroy your soul. He hates you. You must believe it and rise up to take a stand against him.

Most believers today know that something is going wrong in their lives. They know that some force is working against them. Yet they are afraid or ashamed to admit it and seek help. So they pretend it isn't happening and try to go on normally.

God shows us in His Word that this is not the way to solve the problem. We must face the enemy squarely and push him back. Stop hiding your head in the sand. Stop living in a dream world. Stop denying reality. We are in a life and death struggle. The enemy of your soul is at work. We are wrestling against *"principalities, against powers, against the rulers of the darkness of this world, against spiritual wickedness in high places"* (Ephesians 6:12). We need God's help, for we are facing a real enemy.

Our only hope of victory is to *"put on"* Jesus. Only Jesus, living in us, can protect us from the onslaught of the enemy. If Jesus is in you, Satan will have no point of entry to your life. Jesus becomes your shield of faith. His presence protects you from the darts being relentlessly hurled at you by the enemy. Through Him you are able to *"quench"* the fiery darts of the wicked one.

God's Word not only points out the existence of the enemy, It describes him in detail and warns us continually to get ready for battle against him.

This is the same enemy that Jesus had to face:

> *Then was Jesus led up of the Spirit into the wilderness* TO BE TEMPTED OF THE DEVIL.
>
> Matthew 4:1

The apostles were also not immune to Satan's attacks:

> *Wherefore we would have come unto you, even I Paul, once and again; but* SATAN HINDERED US.
>
> 1 Thessalonians 2:18

Even the saints of the Old Testament struggled constantly with this adversary:

> *And he shewed me Joshua the high priest standing before the angel of the Lord, and Satan standing at his right hand* TO RESIST HIM.
>
> Zechariah 3:1

This is not a game. This is serious business. You must wake up. You must be sober. You must be vigilant. Something is happening that will determine your future and the future of your family. You are under attack. The enemy has laid siege to your life.

God warns us to set a guard that will watch for the enemy. People's lives are at stake. We are under attack. The enemy is crouching in the shadows, tracking us like a hungry lion. He is seeking the weak, those who are off guard, those who are unprepared.

Get serious! Satan is after you. If you are not sober and if you are not vigilant, your adversary is going to overcome you. You can count on that.

Why is Satan so angry? Why is he running after you and me? Why does he want to destroy us? Why does he have no mercy, even on innocent little babies? They don't deserve to suffer and die. They don't deserve sickness. They don't deserve pain. But he doesn't care about that. He hates God's creation and is determined to destroy us all.

He is bitter because he once had a place in the heart of God. Before the earth was formed, before the creation of man, God had angels (heavenly spirit beings) that surrounded Him. Their major responsibility was to give Him praise and glory. God set Lucifer to be the head of them. Lucifer was a glorious being. His beauty and his glory resulted in his downfall, for pride entered into his heart.

He saw his worth. He knew his abilities. He gloried in his beauty. He wallowed in his charm. He believed that his wisdom excelled all others. And he said to himself, *"Well, well, well! Now that God has made me an executive and has given me authority, I think I will turn the tables on Him. Yes, I will topple God! Then, everyone will recognize my greatness!"*

God has never been able to tolerate pride. Because of that, Satan was cast out of heaven and, since that day he fell, he has been plotting to get back at God. He hates God with a passion. He hates God's Word. He hates God's Church. He hates God's people. He believes that he has hit on the perfect way to hurt God and get back at Him.

What could be worse for a father than to see his children suffer? What could be worse than to see a child go astray and ruin his life? What could be worse that alienation from a child? These are the thoughts that play on Satan's mind. His delight is to turn God's children away from Him, to cause them to suffer, to lead them into disobedience and alienation from the Father. Satan's highest goal is to destroy God's children totally — body and soul. When he is successful, his cackle of glee rings out through the darkened passages of Hell. He loves it.

Satan knows that he can never defeat God. That's why he picks on us. He knows he will never win in a direct confrontation with the Father, so he goes after the children.

He will use any tactic, try any trick. Nothing is too vile for him. Nothing is too ugly. Nothing is too filthy. He has no pity. He is ruthless and utterly cruel.

Satan knows how much God loves His children. He now knows the great future God has prepared for every one of us. He knows that we are destined for greatness. He knows that we are born to be free. That's why he never stops harassing us. He never lets us rest. He is determined to keep us enslaved. He wants to make us his own children:

The field is the world; the good seed are the children of the kingdom; but the tares are THE CHILDREN OF THE WICKED ONE;

Matthew 13:38

In this the children of God are manifest, and THE CHILDREN OF THE DEVIL: whosoever doeth not righteousness is not of God, neither he that loveth not his brother. 1 John 3:10

Satan is determined to turn believers back. He attacks them relentlessly. Many who have received the Lord as their personal Savior are later heard to say:

"I don't know what is happening to me. It looks like I cannot continue in the faith. I want to serve God, but something is pulling me away from the purpose of God. Something is pulling me away from the service of the Lord. One part of me wants to go to church, while another part of me wants to go find some drugs or something to drink. Something is urging me to do the things which are offensive to God. I want to live right, and I don't understand why I am drawn to do these other things."

When we understand the tactics of a real enemy, it is easy to see why Christians are going through these struggles. Satan knows God's purpose in the life of the believer. Since He doesn't like God, we become his targets too. Since his downfall, he is aware of God's great plans for us. He is jealous of us because we have the blessing of God on our lives. He will do anything and everything to spoil your future. ANYTHING! EVERYTHING! He means business.

We are not dealing with a fool. Satan has been around for a long time. He was created with higher intelligence. He knows what he is doing. When he fell, God took his power from him, but He did not take his ability from him. He still has much of his ability.

Satan is not fooling around because he knows that his time is short. He knows his ultimate end. Hell was not prepared for people, but for Satan and his rebellious troops. It is a place reserved for rebels. Satan knows this and is determined not to go there alone. He is determined to drag down with him as many of God's children as he can. That's why he is chasing you.

You must wake up to this fact. You must get serious. You must be *"on guard."* Satan is stalking you like a lion. He is closing in for the kill. If he can get you in his grasp, he will show no mercy.

Be sober! Be vigilant! We face a real enemy.

Chapter 2

The Tactics Satan Employs

Lest Satan should get an advantage of us: for we are not ignorant of his devices.
2 Corinthians 2:11

In order that Satan might not outwit us. For we are not unaware of his schemes. NIV

Our greatest defense is to know our enemy, to understand his purposes and the tactics he employs to bring them about. If we are ignorant of the *"devices"* of Satan, he can take advantage of us. However, if we are not ignorant of his *"devices,"* he is powerless to harm us. It is that simple.

None of us like to be taken advantage of, yet sometimes it happens. People who don't know how to read and write, for example, are often taken advantage of. Some of them don't know their rights. Some of them are afraid to claim their rights, for some reason.

Another example might be this: a newly-arrived immigrant may be entitled to receive six dollars an hour for his labor. If he hasn't learned the value of the dollar, however, his boss may pay him only two dollars an hour. He might even be happy with that because he doesn't know any better. Unless someone informs him that he is entitled to six dollars an hour, he doesn't know to claim his rightful salary. For the time being, someone is taking advantage of him.

That is exactly what Satan is doing to many people – even to many believers. He may be doing it to you. He may be robbing you blind. You may be settling for second best. You may be missing the mark. You may be entitled to much more than you are receiving. If so, you must first discover his trick. Then you must stand up and demand your rights. You must put the Thief in his place. If you learn his tactics, Satan will have difficulty taking advantage of you.

Satan fears an informed believer. He runs the other way when he sees one. He dreads those who have on spiritual armor. He is a coward. He cowers in fear in the presence of the shield of faith. He knows that his darts are powerless against that shield.

Ignorance is not bliss. Ignorance is tragedy. Ignorance of God's will is the greatest tragedy in life. We must become informed about the important issues of life. If we don't, Satan will cheat us every day.

Many people talk about crooked politicians. They know how to get our money. Others talk about crooked preachers. They know how to get our money. Still others talk about crooked doctors. They know how to get our money. But there is someone far more crooked than any of these. Satan is the Master Deceiver. If you let him do it, he will take you for all you have. We must stop being so gullible, and get smart.

When I was a boy, I loved to trap mice. My father taught me how to do it. I could hear those mice running through our house, especially when the lights were out. If we didn't catch them, they would eat up all the unrefrigerated vegetables we had stored for the family. So before we went to bed, I would set my trap. In the middle of the night, I would hear the trap click and hear the mouse squeak, and I would exalt, *"I've got him! I've got him!"* Sure enough, the next morning I would find a dead mouse in the trap.

I can picture the devil's trap. He has put the finest cheese in it. It is so beautiful! Sometimes he uses the finest fish or the best meat. It is so well placed. He knows what he is doing. He is a practiced hunter. The deception is complete.

A mouse walks by and sees the trap. He senses that it doesn't belong there and is set up just to get him. He says, *"I'm not about to get trapped in there. I'm too clever for that."* And he walks away.

After a few steps, he turns back to see if the cheese is still there. Sure enough! It hasn't moved. *"I know this is a trick,"* he thinks to himself. *"He won't get me. That's for sure."*

He turns again to go, but he catches the smell of it. How alluring! His favorite type of cheese! How did they now? *"I won't be tricked,"* he thinks, *"but it can't hurt anything to stay here for a moment smelling it, can it?"*

He waits for a few moments and nothing happens. No one is watching. He decides to go closer again to inspect it. It still looks like a trap to him, but his desire for the taste of it begins to make him believe that he might outfox the hunter, take the bait, and leave unscathed.

He slowly approaches the bait again. After an agonizing moment of hesitation, he decides that it couldn't hurt to take a little nibble. *"I won't go too far. Just a little! Then, I'll run out of here safely and leave the trap standing empty."*

With the first nibble, he is astonished. He never imagined that any cheese could taste so good. It is delightful! He continues to take small bites around the edges, careful not to set off the dread trap. But, as he savors each delicious morsel, his mind strays more and more from the danger. How could anything that tastes so good be bad? Maybe he has been wrong to be so cautious. This is wonderful!

On occasion, he steps back a bit, as he savors the delicacy, and sees anew the terrible jaws of the trap. Mysteriously, as time progresses, the jaws no longer appear as menacing as before. He grows accustomed to them. He has gone far enough now, with no apparent repercussions, that he begins to feel confident that no harm will come to him. He will not be trapped. He will enjoy his meal and go on his way — as before.

"I'm very clever," he thinks. *"I know how to get what I want without suffering any consequences."* And in this state of self-delusion he works his way into the very center of the bait.

By now, he has had enough for the moment and decides to go tell some of his friends about his good fortune. *"I am such a clever fellow,"* he tells them. *"I know how to fool the trap. I get what I want without being caught."*

And so his fate is sealed. When, after a relatively short time, he feels a renewed desire for the rich bait, he wanders back to the area of the trap. Nothing has changed! Everything is as before! With quiet confidence he thrusts his snout into the juicy tidbit. Then, without warning, the terrible jaws snap shut.

C R A C K!

He cries out for help. When no one seems to hear, he screams. He is in agony. Why can't anyone hear him? He screams louder. At that moment one of his friends wanders by.

"Oh my," he says. *"You are caught in the trap. You were sure this wouldn't happen to you."* Very cautiously he comes nearer and begins to examine the situation.

"Oh, this is the delicacy you told us about," he says as he tastes the bait. *"You were right! This is wonderful!"* And with that he begins eating greedily.

"No!" shouts the trapped mouse. *"What is wrong with you? Can't you see what happened to me? This trap has more than one jaw. Run for your life!"*

But alas, the friend is barely listening. He is enthralled with the tasty bait and is determined to eat his fill. *"This is good cheese,"* he says out of a full mouth. *"Don't worry," I won't get caught."*

Then, **B O O M !** The lights go out.

Satan's snare is so attractive, and playing with it doesn't seem to hurt today. But, believe me, if it doesn't get you today, it will get you tomorrow.

This trap is not just for bad people. Satan loves to catch good people in his trap. He loves to catch young, innocent people in his trap. He loves to catch religious people in his trap. He has some good Baptist people in his trap. He has some good Pentecostal people in his trap. He has some good Methodist people in his trap. In this regard, he is no respecter of persons.

How can good people possibly be trapped in this way? It is because Satan presents such an ingenious deception. It is because he is a master deceiver, a most clever enemy. He knows what he is doing. It is only in mastering his tactics that we can effectively defeat him.

Now that we are aware of the seriousness of this threat, I want to show you in the following pages exactly how Satan thinks and acts. I want to make you aware of his tactics as never before. Open your heart to God and let Him speak to you as you read this book.

Part II

If I Were Satan

Chapter 3

IF I WERE SATAN:
I Would Convince People That I Didn't Even Exist

Satan ... is transformed into an angel of light.
2 Corinthians 11:14

Satan masquerades as an angel of light. NIV

If I were Satan, I would make people believe that I didn't even exist. That sounds crazy, but that is exactly what he is doing to many intellectuals today. They say boldly, "*I don't believe in the devil.*" If you are one of those people, I want to tell you that it doesn't matter what you believe or don't believe; Satan is real and is out to get you.

Our problem today is that we are so well educated. We know so much. We are trained to depend upon our reasoning. We have developed our minds to reason out life's problems. Because the existence of Satan cannot be scientifically proven and isn't logical, many no longer believe that he exists.

Young people are so optimistic these days when they graduate from college. They have the world on a string. They are positive that there is no problem they can't solve. They will always know what to do. Making enough money will resolve all of life's issues; and owning property will make amends for any difficulties encountered along the way.

What a rude awakening they face in the real world! How well Satan has done his work of deception on their minds! He is waiting outside the university entrance to pounce on every young person as they go out the door.

I once heard a wise preacher say, "*If you don't believe there is a devil, try to live one day for God. You will find out quickly that your enemy exists.*" He was right. Satan hates those who try to live for God. He is the enemy of God and the enemy of God's people. If he is not bothering you, it may be because he thinks he already has you in his control.

If you do not believe in a personal devil, you are deceived. This deception is not limited to young people. Older people are also doubting or denying the existence of Satan. Yet his existence is one of the most well documented facts of Scripture. His origins are noted in detail:

> *How art thou fallen from heaven, O Lucifer, son of the morning! how art thou cut down to the ground, which didst weaken the nations! For thou hast said in thine heart, I will ascend into heaven, I will exalt my throne above the stars of God: I will sit also upon the mount of the congregation, in the sides of the north: I will ascend above the heights of the clouds; I will be like the most High. Yet thou shalt be brought down to hell, to the sides of the pit.*
> Isaiah 14:12-15

> *Full of wisdom, and perfect in beauty. Thou hast been in Eden the garden of God; every precious stone was thy covering, the sardius, topaz, and the diamond, the Beryl, the onyx, and the jasper, the sapphire, the emerald, and the carbuncle, and gold: the workmanship of thy tabrets and of thy pipes was prepared in thee in the day that thou wast created. Thou art the anointed cherub that covereth; and I have set thee so: thou wast upon the holy mountain of God; thou hast walked up and down in the midst of the stones of fire. Thou wast perfect in thy ways from the day that thou wast created, till iniquity was found in thee. By the multitude of thy merchandise they have filled the midst of thee with violence, and thou hast sinned: therefore I will cast thee as profane out of the mountain of God: and I*

will destroy thee, O covering cherub, from the midst of the stones of fire. Thine heart was lifted up because of thy beauty, thou hast corrupted thy wisdom by reason of thy brightness: I will cast thee to the ground, I will lay thee before kings, that they may behold thee. Ezekiel 28:12-17

The Bible uses many names to describe Satan. Most of them show us his character. He is "*the accuser.*"

And I heard a loud voice saying in heaven, Now is come salvation, and strength, and the kingdom of our God, and the power of his Christ: for THE ACCUSER of our brethren is cast down, which accused them before our God day and night.
Revelation 12:10

He is the "*adversary.*"

Be sober, be vigilant; because your ADVERSARY the devil, as a roaring lion, walketh about, seeking whom he may devour: 1 Peter 5:8

He is "*the wicked one.*"

When any one heareth the word of the kingdom, and understandeth it not, then cometh THE WICKED ONE, and catcheth away that which was sown in his heart. Matthew 13:19

He is "*the tempter.*"

And when THE TEMPTER came to him, he said, If thou be the Son of God, command that these stones be made bread. Matthew 4:3

He is *"the god of this world."*

In whom THE GOD OF THIS WORLD hath blinded the minds of them which believe not, lest the light of the glorious gospel of Christ, who is the image of God, should shine unto them.
2 Corinthians 4:4

He is *"the prince of the power of the air."*

Wherein in time past ye walked according to the course of this world, according to THE PRINCE OF THE POWER OF THE AIR, the spirit that now worketh in the children of disobedience:
Ephesians 2:2

He is a *"murderer."* But, above all, he is *"a liar."*

Ye are of your father the devil, and the lusts of your father ye will do. He was a MURDERER from the beginning, and abode not in the truth, because there is no truth in him. When he speaketh a lie, he speaketh of his own: for HE IS A LIAR, and the father of it. John 8:44

Satan is a confirmed liar. He never tells the truth about himself. A murderer doesn't tell the truth. A thief doesn't tell the truth. How can we expect Satan to tell the truth? He is the *"father"* of lies.

He never identifies himself as the tempter. He never calls himself a deceiver. He doesn't want us to know that he is the evil one.

Satan never tells the whole truth. He may tell you a half truth. When part of what he says is correct, you may accept the rest of his line. You can be sure most of it will turn out to be lies. Satan never tells the truth. You may reach a conclusion from what Satan has told you, but your conclusion is a deception. You may sincerely believe that you are right, but you may be sincerely wrong. Satan is a liar. Why should we ever trust him?

It was Satan's lies to Adam and Eve which caused their downfall. He cleverly convinced then to disobey God. They were not unintelligent people. They were created in the image of God and walked and talked with God. They were deceived because Satan's lie to them was very clever:

> *"God told you that you would die if you ate of that tree. Isn't that just like God? He is so mischievous. He knows that if you eat of that tree, you will become as great as He is; and He is jealous of the thought. Look at this fruit. Does this look like it would kill you? This is wonderful fruit. Believe me. Here, eat some. You'll see what I'm talking about."*

The Scriptures tell it like this:

And the serpent said unto the woman, Ye shall not surely die: For God doth know that in the day ye eat thereof, then your eyes shall be opened, and ye shall be as gods, knowing good and evil. And when the woman saw that the tree was good for food, and that it was pleasant to the eyes, and a tree to be desired to make one wise, she took of the fruit thereof, and did eat, and gave also unto her husband with her; and he did eat.

Genesis 3:4-6

What a master deceiver Satan is! He can make people believe anything. He even convinces people that he doesn't exist.

If I were Satan, I would never appear as a devil or an evil being. I would disguise myself as a friend, or someone who is truly concerned with people's problems. I would appear as an *"angel of light."* And that is exactly what he does.

If I were Satan, I would do exactly what he is doing.

Chapter 4

IF I WERE SATAN:
I Would Work On People's Feelings and Thoughts

For as he thinketh in his heart, so is he:
Proverbs 23:7

If I were Satan I would work on your feelings. I would work on the way you think. I would know what you want, and I would give you what you want — until I had you in my power. This is Satan's ultimate goal. He intends to make you his child and to cause you to serve him totally.

I don't know anyone who wants to be an alcoholic, but there are many alcoholics these days. People become alcoholics because they are deceived. Satan gets control of their feelings and of their thought life.

So many people get hooked on drugs. They think, "*I can stop it when I want to.*" They are deceived. Once they are hooked and are no longer free to make their own decisions, they begin to sell everything they own and, when that is all gone, to steal anything they can lay their hands on to satisfy that craving. Their thought life has come under Satan's control, slowly but surely — until it's too late.

Good women are having abortions. They are deceived into thinking they are doing the correct thing. They are convinced that this is not only their "*right,*" but that it is "*right.*"

This type of deception doesn't happen overnight. Little by little Satan gains control of people's emotions and of their thoughts, until he has them under his power. Most people don't even know what is happening.

Satan is so clever. He knows exactly what he is doing.

When most people are caught in their crime or their vice, they invariably say:

"*I didn't mean to go that far.*"
"*I wish I hadn't gone that far.*"
"*I was trapped.*"
"*I couldn't help myself.*"

People do become powerless to help themselves when they have fallen into the snare of the enemy.

Step by tiny step he gets control of their lives, without them even being aware that he is at work.

What ingenious deceit! Satan knows that if he controls the thought life, he controls the man. If he controls the thought life, he controls the woman.

Once Satan takes control of a person's thoughts and emotions, he tells them the most horrible lies because he is shameless.

He tells people that once they are bound, there is no way for them to be freed. He tells them that there is no escape, no way out. He makes them feel hopeless and helpless. He makes them believe that God doesn't love them anymore and that they have done things so terrible that they can never be forgiven.

All the while, the Father stands with His arms extended calling to His errant children:

> *Behold, I stand at the door, and knock: if any man hear my voice, and open the door, I will come in to him, and will sup with him, and he with me.*
>
> Revelation 3:20

He is saying:

> *Whosoever shall call on the name of the Lord shall be saved.* Acts 2:21

He is the loving Father who welcomes home the prodigal son with rejoicing:

> *But when he was yet a great way off, his father saw him, and had compassion, and ran, and fell on his*

> *neck, and kissed him. And the son said unto him, Father, I have sinned against heaven, and in thy sight, and am no more worthy to be called thy son. But the father said to his servants, Bring forth the best robe, and put it on him; and put a ring on his hand, and shoes on his feet: And bring hither the fatted calf, and kill it; and let us eat, and be merry: For this my son was dead, and is alive again; he was lost, and is found. And they began to be merry.*
>
> Luke 15:21-24

To keep men from hearing the Father's voice of love, Satan never ceases to repeat his lies to those whom he has trapped. *"There is no escape from the downward pull to doom. There is no way out,"* he says. He even puts the blame on God and makes people angry and resentful with their loving Creator. Satan tries to make people believe that God acts in His own interests, that He has forgotten them and forsaken them. *"When God acts,"* he tells them, *"it is in favor of a selective group."*

In this way, Satan makes people bitter against God and their fellow man. He is the master deceiver, with centuries of experience to hone his trade.

If I were Satan, I would do exactly what he is doing.

Chapter 5

IF I WERE SATAN:
I Would Make Sin Very, Very Attractive

By faith Moses, when he was come to years, refused to be called the son of Pharaoh's daughter; Choosing rather to suffer affliction with the people of God, than to enjoy the pleasures of sin for a season; Hebrews 11:24-25

He chose to be mistreated along with the people of God rather than to enjoy the pleasures of sin for a short time. NIV

If I were Satan, I would make sin look so attractive. I would do a complete public relations campaign, going to great lengths to convince people that sin is beautiful; sin is great; sin brings happiness; and sin bears no consequences. I would make sin so lovely that it would cause the eyes of men to lust after evil. They would be ready to pay any price for it.

I would never let them know that sin is disobeying the Word of God. I would gloss over the fact that sin is displeasing to God, breaks the heart of God, and demands that He respond with correction. I would cause them to forget the words of sacred Scripture:

> *The soul that sinneth, it shall die.* Ezekiel 18:4

> *For the wages of sin is death; but the gift of God is eternal life through Jesus Christ our Lord.*
> Romans 6:23

I would actually take the word "*sin*" out of some dictionaries and replace it with "more positive" and lovely words. In everyday conversation, I would change the word "*adultery*" into "*meaningful relationship.*" I would change "*homosexuality*" into "*alternate lifestyle.*" I would make alcoholism a sickness. I would make sin so attractive that people would like it.

This is exactly what Satan is doing. He is deceiving the people of all nations. Then, when he has deceived a person and convinced them to yield to him, he stands behind them and roars with laughter:

"Ha! Ha! Ha! Ha! I got him. I got him! I knew I would get him! I knew it all the time! What a dope! He fell for it! I told you I would get him! It was only a matter of time! I am a genius."

All the demons join this satanic rejoicing:

"You got him! What a sap! He was doomed from the beginning!"

Have you ever been approached by those who sell fake Rolex watches? In fact, they look like a Rolex, but they don't cost thousands of dollars (as does a real Rolex). They are much cheaper because they are fakes. Many people buy these fake watches because they are so beautiful. Satan is like the champion fake Rolex salesman. He is selling his line successfully to millions of otherwise intelligent people.

We need to wake up! We need to put a stop to this! We need to take a stand against this deceit! Unless we say "no" to the devil and to sin, he will reign over our homes. He will reign over our families. He will reign over our churches. When we say *"yes"* to sin, we lose control over our lives and hand authority to Satan.

Sin has become so attractive today that we find it in every neighborhood. Neighbors are fighting each other. Knives are pulled in the street, as tempers flare. Some of those same people go to church and act very holy on Sunday.

Sin has become so attractive today that we find it in the church. We have pews filled with hypocrites who refuse to hear the Word of God, refuse to shake hands with one another, and refuse to let God change their lives. *"If I die, don't come to my funeral,"* they say. *"I am going home."* I would like to ask those people a question: *"Which home are they going to?"* They certainly aren't going to God's home. No sin will enter there.

> *But the fearful, and unbelieving, and abominable, and murderers, and whoremongers, and sorcerers, and idolaters, and all liars, shall have their part in the lake which burneth with fire and brimstone: which is the second death.* Revelation 21:8

Sin has affected our families – our brothers and sisters, our children. If we want to see the glory of God and the peace of God returned to our families, we must take a stand against the enemy who is devastating our loved ones.

Believers have compromised so much with sin that when the Word of God is preached and begins to prick their hearts, their response is, *"No! No! Not yet!"* Some find sin so attractive that they respond with anger and go out the door of the church, vowing never to return.

When God deals with us about sin, it is because He wants to set us free. The devil tells us to get up and leave the church at such moments. He tells us never to go back. He doesn't want us to get God's Word in our hearts. He wants to see us destroyed. But we cannot live without the Word of God. Satan's way is not satisfying. He has come only to steal, kill and destroy. We need God's blessing. His ways are life. Satan only offers death.

> *The thief cometh not, but for to steal, and to kill, and to destroy: I am come that they might have life, and that they might have it more abundantly.*
>
> John 10:10

When God begins to work in your heart, the devil will start making you uncomfortable. He's scared. He doesn't want the Holy Spirit talking to you. He doesn't want you to hear the truth. He wants you to be offended and storm off. Then, he'll win.

Don't be a fool. God's Word is true:

> *Be not deceived; God is not mocked: for whatsoever a man soweth, that shall he also reap.*
>
> Galatians 6:7

Don't be deceived. Recognize sin for what it is. Don't break the Father's heart by playing around with the enemy. Get on God's side and get victory over sin and the Devil.

Chapter 6

IF I WERE SATAN:
I Would Hinder the Effect of the Word of God

And he spake many things unto them in parables, saying, Behold, a sower went forth to sow; And when he sowed, some seeds fell by the way side, and the fowls came and devoured them up: Some fell upon stony places, where they had not much earth: and forthwith they sprung up, because they had no deepness of earth: And when the sun was up, they were scorched; and because they had no root, they withered away. And some fell among thorns; and

> *the thorns sprung up, and choked them: But other fell into good ground, and brought forth fruit, some an hundredfold, some sixtyfold, some thirtyfold. Who hath ears to hear, let him hear.*
>
> Matthew 13:3-9

If I were Satan, I would do everything I could to hinder the Word of God. Many believers still do not understand: that the Word of God is *"powerful and sharper than any two-edged sword."*

> *For the word of God is quick, and powerful, and sharper than any twoedged sword, piercing even to the dividing asunder of soul and spirit, and of the joints and marrow, and is a discerner of the thoughts and intents of the heart.*
>
> Hebrews 4:12

Satan knows that in order for him to defeat God's plans for His people, the Word must be hindered. If the Word is allowed to sink into the hearts of men, it will bring deliverance to them – deliverance from sin, from sickness, from infirmity, and from pain. The very thought is frightening to our enemy. The Word has power to destroy his entire kingdom. He is determined that It not be given free course.

Just as in the parable of the sower, I could think of a number of ways to hinder the effect of the Word – if I were Satan.

If I were Satan, I would tell sinners that the Bible is so holy that they dare not touch it until they get right with God. That is a lie. If you begin to open the Bible, you will get right with God. Don't let the sin in your life hinder you from searching God's Word. If you read the Bible, you will learn how to overcome sin. The Bible will teach you how to live right.

If I were Satan, I would tell people that the Bible is so holy, they should show respect for it by putting it under their pillow at night as protection from demons. Then, before they sleep, they can say:

> *"Now I lay me down to sleep, I pray the Lord my soul to keep."*

Many people are not taking the Word of God any more seriously than that. But God didn't intend for His Word to be under your pillow. He intended for It to be in your heart.

Some people haven't used their Bible for so long that they don't know where it is. It is on some shelf collecting dust or packed away in some suitcase – somewhere. Satan loves that. He doesn't want you to put on the whole armor of God. He wants you to be weak against his advances.

If I were Satan, I would convince people to limit the study of the Bible to Sunday morning church services. There was a time, in the Church of England (which later became the Anglican Church), when the Bible was chained to the pulpit. It was so costly and so scarce that anyone who wanted to read It had to come to the church. It could not be taken out.

Although the Bible is now available to every believer, that same thing is happening today. The devil is tying the Word of God to the church. He is making people believe that it is only during the time they are in the church building that they should concentrate on the Word of God. The Word is not going out with people. It is not going into their hearts. Many believers never open the Bible during the week. They are deceived and robbed of Its benefits.

If I were Satan, I would get very busy when God began to minister to peoples' hearts in the services. I would tell them that the message was for someone else – the person beside them, or someone who didn't even attend church that day, anyone else – but not for them personally.

I would try to make people forget the message even before they get out the door. I would change their thoughts to other things. I would remind them of bills to be paid, jobs to be done, problems to be solved, or of good food waiting to be eaten. I would use other people to spread gossip right there in the aisles of the church and change the subject to scandalous things that happen in the community – anything to cause them to forget the Word. I would make them like the rocks upon which the seed couldn't find root. I would make them like a trodden path, too hardened to give place to the seed.

Why would Satan go to all this trouble over an old book? I want to tell you: That *"Old Book"* has power. It is the living Word of God, divinely inspired.

All scripture is given by inspiration of God, and is profitable for doctrine, for reproof, for correction, for instruction in righteousness:

2 Timothy 3:16

That divinely inspired Word has power to keep you from sin:

Thy word have I hid in mine heart, that I might not sin against thee. Psalms 119:11

That God-breathed Word has power to heal your sick body:

He sent his word, and healed them, and delivered them from their destructions. Psalms 107:20

If you are a sinner, that Word will help you to be born again and become a child of God:

Being born again, not of corruptible seed, but of incorruptible, by the word of God, which liveth and abideth for ever. 1 Peter 1:23

That Word has power to help you overcome the Wicked One:

I have written unto you, young men, because ye are strong, and the word of God abideth in you, and ye have overcome the wicked one. 1 John 2:14

No wonder Satan hates the Word of God!

If I were Satan, I would tell people not to pay too much attention to the preacher. After all, they know the Word for themselves. They don't need anyone else to interpret it for them. If people know the Word so well, I wonder why they don't live by the Word!

I would cause people to enjoy the choir more than they enjoy the preaching of the Word. I would cause them to flock to the church when a visiting choir or a well-known musician is coming. Then, I would put some hypocrites in the choir. When they took off their choir robes, they would be something different underneath.

If I were Satan, I would cause religious people to go to church only on special occasions – such as Christmas, New Years Eve, Easter, Mother's Day, Father's Day, or for funeral services.

Satan is happy when we restrict church attendance to these special occasions. It works in his favor.

If I were Satan, I would do exactly what he is doing.

Chapter 7

IF I WERE SATAN:
I Would Cause People To Reject the Holy Spirit

But ye shall receive power, after that the Holy Ghost is come upon you: and ye shall be witnesses unto me both in Jerusalem, and in all Judaea, and in Samaria, and unto the uttermost part of the earth. Acts 1:8

But you will receive power when the Holy Spirit comes on you; and you will be my witnesses in Jerusalem, and in all Judea and Samaria, and to the ends of the earth. NIV

If I were Satan, I would tell people not to believe in the Holy Ghost and all the supernatural manifestations that accompany the Holy Ghost (also know as the Holy Spirit). *"That's crazy!"* I would tell them. *"Speaking in tongues? Come on! We are living in the closing days of the twentieth century. Don't talk about that dark ages stuff."*

I would convince people that speaking in tongues passed away with the death of the first century Apostles.

I would tell people how important it is to stand on their religious traditions and ignore anything in the Bible that isn't included.

Satan knows that if believers never speak in tongues they will never achieve the fullness of the power promised by God. The devil doesn't want believers to have power. He doesn't want them to be witnesses. He doesn't want the Gospel to be preached in the whole world. He doesn't want believers to pray in the Spirit, walk in the Spirit and live in the Spirit.

If I were Satan, I would tell people:

> *"Don't believe that teaching about speaking in tongues. That is dangerous. Anyone who speaks in tongues has some mental problem. They probably even have some demon."*

I would cause believers to ignore what the Bible says about speaking in tongues:

> *For if I pray in an unknown tongue, my spirit prayeth.* 1 Corinthians 14:14

The devil doesn't want believers to know that *"my spirit prays"* when I am praying in tongues. He is afraid that we will become too spiritual and will walk in the power of God. He will do anything to see that we keep walking in the flesh.

If I were him, I would convince ministers to forbid speaking in tongues in the church, ignoring what the Bible says:

> *Wherefore, brethren, covet to prophesy, and forbid not to speak with tongues.*
>
> 1 Corinthians 14:39

Why does the Bible warn us not to forbid the speaking in tongues? Because such great power is released when we speak in the Spirit that Satan gets scared. He doesn't want you to be speaking a heavenly language. He doesn't want you to know and understand the things of God.

Before I received the gift of the Holy Ghost and spoke in tongues, I was scared of the devil. Anytime I saw something that resembled his work, I ran away. But since I received the gift of the Holy Ghost, he is SCARED of me. When I get on my knees and open my mouth to pray, he says:

> *"Look out! Here comes that man of God. Look out! Here comes that one who will not compromise with me. Here comes that one that will not allow me to torment him. He is coming to lash at me again."*

I have learned the secrets of overcoming Satan. I obey the Bible. I submit myself to God through the Spirit. Then, when I resist him, he runs away from me. God said:

> *Submit yourselves therefore to God. Resist the devil, and he will flee from you.* James 4:7

Praise God! I love His Word. It gives me power over the Wicked One. I refuse to listen to his lies against the Holy Ghost. It was the power of the Holy Ghost that made the disciples successful. When Jesus was taken from the earth and had gone to present Himself and to take His place with the Father, the disciples were left alone.

They were very common people, but they had the privilege of being with Jesus for more than three years. They had seen Him change the lives of sinners. They had seen Him heal the blind. They had seen Him make the crippled walk. They had even seen Him raise the dead.

Jesus had promised them that He would never forsake them. Now, He had gone back physically to heaven, and they were alone. But Jesus was true to His Word. He sent them the Comforter. Through the Holy Ghost, He was with them to confirm the Word they preached everywhere in His name.

And it worked. Peter and John, who were uneducated fishermen, were going to the Temple to pray when they met a crippled man begging for money. I love what Peter told him:

> *Then Peter said, Silver and gold have I none; but such as I have give I thee: In the name of Jesus Christ of Nazareth rise up and walk.* Acts 3:6

These men were not intimidated by the power of Satan to cripple and destroy. They had Jesus living in them. He was in their hearts and on their lips. He was their shield of faith.

> *And he took him by the right hand, and lifted him up: and immediately his feet and ancle bones received strength.* Acts 3:7

Who told Peter what to do to help the man be delivered? He didn't have a Ph.D., but he had the Holy Ghost. The Holy Ghost will give you wisdom and show you exactly what to do in any given situation. If the Holy Ghost is working in you, something supernatural will happen every time you call upon the name of Jesus.

The reason most Christians are being constantly battered by the enemy is that they are afraid of the Holy Ghost. Many believers run away from Him. The way He does things is strange to them. When He begins to move, they begin to get nervous. They don't know what is happening. They don't realize that the Holy Ghost is the Energizer.

You can't stand still when the Energizer starts moving. You can't keep quite when the Energizer is moving. The Holy Spirit is our Energizer. Let Him energize YOU.

When the work of the first century church grew and more workers were needed, the Apostles instructed the people to search for those with special qualifications:

> *Wherefore, brethren, look ye out among you seven men of honest report, full of the Holy Ghost and wisdom, whom we may appoint over this business.*
> Acts 6:3

The work of the Church demands men and women full of the Spirit. Seven men were chosen to help the apostles.

> *And the saying pleased the whole multitude: and they chose Stephen, a man full of faith and of the Holy Ghost, and Philip, and Prochorus, and Nicanor, and Timon, and Parmenas, and Nicolas a proselyte of Antioch:* Acts 6:5

One of the seven men chosen was Stephen. He became a giant of faith and the first Christian martyr. He was *"a man full of faith and of the Holy Ghost."*

The Holy Ghost can make you a giant of faith. With the power of the Holy Ghost, you can overcome the enemy. Because the power of the Holy Ghost was in Stephen, he *"did great wonders."*

> *And Stephen, full of faith and power, did great wonders and miracles among the people.*
> Acts 6:8

If God could make Stephen an overcomer, He can make you an overcomer. If Stephen could do great wonders and miracles, you can do great wonders and miracles also — through the power of the Holy Spirit.

When the disciples had chosen these men and had placed them in positions of responsibility, something wonderful happened in Jerusalem:

> *And the word of God increased; and the number of the disciples multiplied in Jerusalem greatly; and a great company of the priests were obedient to the faith.*
> Acts 6:7

The priests originally believed that the Christians were out of their minds. They rejected their preaching concerning Jesus. In fact, they took some of these preachers and put them in prison. They whipped them and disgraced them openly. But, when the Word of God increased and people full of the Holy Ghost were taking responsibility, the priests could no longer deny the power of Jesus. They accepted the Gospel. That's what the power of the Holy Ghost does.

Many churches today wonder why their young people are straying into the world. At the same time, they have nothing but criticism for the Holy Ghost. Many parents are devastated when their young daughters don't come home on Saturday night, yet they keep criticizing the Holy Ghost. Many mothers weep bitter tears because their teenagers are experimenting with drugs, yet they keep criticizing the Holy Ghost.

The Holy Ghost gives us power to live the Christian life. The Holy Ghost gives us power to overcome sin. The Holy Ghost gives us power against the enemy of our souls. Stop criticizing the Holy Ghost and let Him do things the way He wants to do them.

When I was a boy, I overheard some of my closest friends criticizing their Spirit-filled parents and other Christians. Like most children, I wanted to please the crowd, so I joined in. I criticized my own father and mother. I made fun of the laying on of hands and of speaking in tongues. Everyone laughed with me.

When I got saved and filled with the Spirit, God reminded me of that behavior and convicted me, so I had to go to my parents and ask their forgiveness. *"Daddy, Mama,"* I said, *"if you were crazy for believing, receiving and acting on the leading of the Holy Spirit, then I have just joined you."*

As I continued to grow up, my family was so grateful to God that I had not become one of the wayward boys of the community. I have praised God myself many times that He saved me from all the things the other boys my age were doing. I could have gotten into drugs or many other evil things. Thank God I got into the Holy Ghost and said, *"Father, all that I want to do with my life is to live it for You. I don't have time to play games. I mean business."*

More than twenty years have gone by, but I still get excited about each new day. The Holy Ghost is a wonderful Keeper, a wonderful Guardian. I know that many good things are yet to come and I have never regretted my decision to serve the Lord and be a man of the Spirit — even for one day.

When sick people need my help, I call on that Friend I met over twenty years ago. He always answers. When I say, *"Jesus, I know that You love sick people, and I am believing You to heal this person,"* He reaches down in compassion and does the work. That's what the Holy Ghost does for you.

When I see blind people, I say, *"God, look at them. You didn't create them blind. The devil has made them blind. Oh God, open their eyes — in the name of Jesus."* He answers my prayer and opens their eyes. That's what the Holy Ghost will do for you.

Four times I have seen God raise the dead. One of those raised was my own wife. That's what the Holy Ghost can do for you.

Having experienced all this, should I now turn my back on the Holy Ghost and believe Satan's lies? Should I believe that the age of the Holy Spirit has passed and that the world has more to offer me now? Never! The world has nothing that interests me. I am dead to the world and alive in the Spirit of God.

If you want to walk in the power of God and you want to see the working of the Spirit of God, then get out of the influence of the world into the Spirit.

> *Love not the world, neither the things that are in the world. If any man love the world, the love of the Father is not in him.* 1 John 2:15

Those priests, when they heard the Gospel, got out of their dead religious system. They decided to follow the truth. They knew that the truth *"will set you free"* (John 8:32).

Why is it that church buildings are on sale in the Western countries? Why is it that pews are on sale? Is it not because we have abandoned the Holy Ghost?

In the place where I was born in Africa, most of us didn't have a church building. Some people lived in tents. Some worshiped in the open field. But, rain or shine, we gathered to honor and worship the Lord for hours. The believers of the so-called "third-world" wouldn't know what to do without the Holy Ghost.

In our African culture, people are so susceptible to evil influence that they are naturally sensitive to spiritual things. We are not also technically influenced to forget the things of the Spirit world. Men and women of all denominations and churches believe in the Spirit and speak in tongues. The coming of Western missionaries many times has served to move people away from the simplicity of their faith into doctrinal fallacy.

Jesus was gone when Stephen performed his miracles. He could have said, *"He's gone. The One we trusted is gone."* But he knew the promises of God: Even if He is gone physically, His power is with us through the Holy Spirit.

Jesus didn't say He would let the enemy ride roughshod over us. He said not to worry because He would never leave us. That presence is in the Holy Ghost. Don't reject Him!

God is still doing miracles through His people — by the Holy Spirit. People of God can still overcome the wicked one — by the Holy Spirit. Get involved! Don't be afraid of the Spirit of God! Let Him do His work in you. Don't be held back by tradition. Let the Spirit have His way!

How terrible that men fear the Holy Ghost more than they fear Satan! How terrible that men revere Satan more than the Holy Ghost! How terrible that we don't hesitate to get close to Satan, but we hesitate to draw nearer to the Spirit of God! How terrible that we are more sensitive to what Satan wants of us than we are of the Spirit's will for our lives!

These are all the result of Satan's deceptions. He is busy, faithfully doing his work.

Christians are frightened of what the Spirit of God wants them to do. They say, *"I'm not ready yet."* They are more ready to work for the devil than they are to work for God.

I have heard people say:

"I am not ready."
"I am afraid."
"There are some things that I cannot let go of."
"I want to serve God, but I am scared."
"Don't you understand?"

I do understand. I understand who they are honoring and revering. I understand that they are being deceived. I understand that they are being taken for a ride. I understand that they are headed for certain destruction.

Another tactic of Satan is to imitate the Holy Ghost. A false wind is blowing in the Church. Satan is trying to imitate the wind of the Holy Ghost. He is blowing with destruction upon all those who will accept his deceit. Be aware of what he is doing. There is no substitute for the power of the Holy Spirit.

Several years ago a young man from Georgia came into the church I am pastoring. He was drunk. He sat in the front row and went to sleep. His snoring disturbed some people. When I began preaching, he woke up, rose to his feet and tried to interrupt me. The Holy Ghost gave me wisdom to deal with him. *"If you will wait until I finish,"* I told him, *"I will answer all your questions."*

When I finished preaching, he was again deep in sleep. I was led of the Spirit to approach him. I pulled him to his feet and tried to shake him awake. I finally got him to put his hands up. He was still groggy. When we laid hands on him, the power of the Holy Ghost touched him and he was slain in the Spirit. He didn't know what was happening to him.

After he lay there for a while, he got up, shook his head, and shouted, *"God is real."* His drunkenness was gone instantly. He was a new and sober man — totally set free.

After he went back to Georgia, he called me almost every day for a while. Then, he decided to move to North Carolina so that he could attend our church and grow in the Lord. That's what the Holy Ghost can do for you.

Long ago I made up my mind that no man would ever make me deny the power of the Holy Ghost. No way! With many people it happens so gradually they don't realize what is taking place.

An illiterate lady from East Africa was so anointed of the Lord that when the sick stood in the spot where she had been standing or touched something that she had recently touched they were healed. When an American evangelist visited her country, someone told him about her. He was so impressed that he decided to take her to Europe and America and let people see what God was doing through her. In the process, pride crept in, the lady lost that glorious anointing, and never recovered it.

I remember the story of a daughter of a Christian man who drew near to him one day, put her head on his chest, and looked up into his eyes. *"Daddy,"* she asked, *"is God dead?"*

The father was stunned. *"Of course not,"* he answered. *"God's not dead. Why would you ask me such a question?"*

The sincerity of the little girl struck the man as she replied, *"You act like He's dead. I never hear you praise Him anymore. I never hear you talk about His love anymore."*

That's what's wrong with most of us. We think God is dead because believers are so silent. Because many believers have denied the Holy Ghost, we think that God is not moving as He once did. It isn't God that is at fault. It is the fault of those who have neglected His Spirit.

When there was a spiritual need in the Church, the disciples didn't form committees to solve the problems.

They looked for men full of the Holy Ghost. I understand why Satan tells people that this Holy Ghost business is crazy stuff. He knows that we can change the world with God's power – manifested through the Holy Spirit.

Make a firm commitment to God today to never be ashamed of His Spirit and to allow the Holy Ghost to totally control your life in every way. When you make that commitment, Satan becomes powerless to touch your life.

Chapter 8

IF I WERE SATAN:
I Would Insist That Healing Is Not For An Enlightened Age

How God anointed Jesus of Nazareth with the Holy Ghost and with power: who went about doing good, and healing all that were oppressed of the devil; for God was with him. Acts 10:38

How God anointed Jesus of Nazareth with the Holy Spirit and power, and how he went around doing good and healing all who were under the power of the devil, because God was with him. NIV

If I were Satan, I would tell people that divine healing has no place in an enlightened society. We are too advanced for that. We are too well educated for that. I would tell them that healing can be dismissed just as easily as other superstitions that uneducated people have held down through the centuries.

I would say to people, *"Friend, don't believe in that healing stuff. It's crazy. Forget it!"*

I would tell people that sickness is just a normal part of life and that Christians should expect to be sick just as much as non-Christians.

I would tell them that sickness is really good because it causes them to be more humble. I would tell people that when they come to church sick they should just be spiritual about it, accept it, and thank God for it. They should go about declaring:

> *"Praise God! Hallelujah! My arthritis has flared up, but thank God it makes me humble."*

I would tell people that anyone who has a life-threatening disease shouldn't believe God for healing because if they pass on from here, they go to be with the Lord anyway.

If I were Satan, I would tell people that their bladder problem, their rheumatism, or their hemorrhoids should just be accepted as part of the cross that God wants them to bear. Some people say:

> *"I'm on that journey, and I've got to bear afflictions. But who knows? The good Lord*

> *understands. The sicker I get, the closer I get to the good Lord."*

Beloved, I don't believe what I see happening to Christians today. If God, our Father, Who loves us as sons and daughters, would purposely make us sick, then we have no business following Him. Sickness is not of God. If it were of God, then Jesus would have come to earth promoting sickness. He didn't. He went about destroying sickness.

If I were Satan, I would tell people that there are certain cases that God cannot heal. If the doctor cannot do anything, then no one can do anything. I would make people believe that AIDS victims can never be cured by God, that AIDS is God's way of disciplining them, and that God has sentenced them to death. I would tell people that if they get sick because of sin, God will never heal them — neither in this life nor in the life to come. I would do everything in my power to make people feel unworthy of God's healing power in their lives.

If I were Satan, I would tell people that anything destructive and evil which happens is already programmed by God. There is nothing you can do about it. Whether it seems good or bad to you, accept it as from the Lord.

I would tell people:

> *"Just take it easy. Don't worry about a thing. If something seems to be going wrong in your life, just give it time to take care of itself. Almost everything*

> *heals itself in time. Who knows? In a day 'bye and bye' God will give everyone solace. You are just walking 'on the rough side of the mountain.' Things will get better without you having to intervene. When you have been so long 'on the rough side of the mountain,' you will surely come out on the plain. Relax."*

I would lead everyone to misuse the Scriptures in Job, and I would let them identify with Job. *"Who knows?"* some people say. *"I am like Job. God is using this trial to train me."* Train you for what?

When the devil wanted to hinder Job, God didn't give him a green light to destroy His servant. He said, *"Go ahead, Satan, because Job will not worship you. He will not side with you. He will be faithful to Me."* God didn't expect Job to believe everything the devil said. He expected His servant to believe what His heavenly Father told him.

It wasn't God that afflicted Job; it was Satan. God granted him permission to test Job.

If I were Satan, I would tell you that healing is not for today, that the day of miracles is passed, and that we are not to expect the same things experienced by the first-century church.

This is a particularly vicious lie, for if the age of miracles is passed, then salvation by faith in the sacrifice of Jesus (that greatest of all miracles) is also passed. The age of miracles is not passed, and God is still saving and still healing.

Several years ago, when my oldest daughter, Anna-Kissel, was just a year old, she became very ill. Her face turned red when she cried one day for about fifteen minutes. We noticed her discomfort, and when her diaper was changed, we found that she had such severe constipation that she was bleeding from the bowels.

I could have said that God wanted to teach us something or that He was using our child's suffering to make us humble, or that this experience was good for our souls. But I knew that wasn't the case.

I said, *"No! This is not from God. This is Satan's work."* (Only the devil would afflict an innocent child.) I put my hands on that precious girl, and I said, *"Devil, you know that you are trespassing. You know that you have no right in my house. Who asked you to come here? Get out."*

My daughter looked at me and smiled; and I said to my wife, *"Honey, she's all right. Get a new diaper for her."* When the diaper was in place, the child got up to play. She was healed.

Some people would have said, *"Well, who knows? Maybe the good Lord wants to teach me patience."*

Now, think about that. My baby is sick, my baby is in pain. And God wants to teach me a lesson by that? Are these people serious? If that is the case, then Jesus made a big mistake by preaching healing. He healed the sick.

> *And they brought unto him all sick people that were taken with divers diseases and torments, and those which were possessed with devils, and those which*

> *were lunatick, and those that had the palsy; and HE HEALED THEM.* Matthew 4:24
>
> *When the even was come, they brought unto him many that were possessed with devils: and he cast out the spirits with his word, and HEALED ALL THAT WERE SICK:* Matthew 8:16
>
> *But when Jesus knew it, he withdrew himself from thence: and great multitudes followed him, and HE HEALED THEM ALL;* Matthew 12:15

The devil doesn't want you to believe that God wants to heal ALL. He will do anything to convince you that your case is different and that God can't help you.

If I were Satan, I would present half-truths on healing. I would remind people how Brother or Sister So-and-So died without receiving miraculous healing from God. *"Are you better than other believers?"* I would ask. I would use this to cause division in the church.

Get God's Word deep into your heart. Resist the lies of Satan and receive the miracle God has for your life.

Chapter 9

IF I WERE SATAN:
I Would Cause Christians To Murmur

And in those days, when the number of the disciples was multiplied, there arose a murmuring of the Grecians against the Hebrews, because their widows were neglected in the daily ministration.

Acts 6:1

If I were Satan, I would do exactly what he did in the Church at Jerusalem. He was jealous because the disciples had the power of God. He was jealous because they were so joyful. He was jealous because they were growing and prospering. He was angry because they had liberty. He despised the excitement which he witnessed on the faces of the people. He had to do something. His kingdom was suffering defeat.

He couldn't get the apostles to get drunk or to leave their wives, so he tried to discourage them through persecution. But that didn't work. Persecution only strengthened the Church. He finally hit on a scheme. He would play on the sentiments of the people. He would exploit the racial differences in their midst. He would exploit the needs of the widows. He would cause the people to murmur.

Murmuring has been one of the most effective tools of the enemy down through the centuries. It takes many forms. There is too much murmuring among families.

My heart goes out to young people today. Some of them have great potential. But, instead of achieving their potential and being blessed of God, they are "messed up" and confused. They have good jobs and make big money, but the day after payday they are broke. Their arms are covered with needle tracks. They are experimenting with drugs.

These young people and some executives are deceived. They believe that they have discovered an "alternative life style." The truth is that they are in total bondage to the devil.

When they confide in their parents (thinking that Mama and Papa will surely have an answer, will surely lend a sympathetic ear, and will surely do something constructive), parents don't know what to do, so they go throughout the neighborhood telling everyone about it. They go from door to door, neighbor to neighbor, relative to relative, and friend to friend, murmuring about what bad children they have.

When the children know that their parents have gossiped their problems around, they are crushed. They confront their parents:

> *"Mama, what's this all about? Daddy, what's this all about? You say you are Christians. You say you believe in God. I thought you were going to help me. What are you doing to help me? Nothing! All you do is talk about me. All you do is go around the neighborhood and tell everyone how bad I am. All you can do about my problem is murmur."*

Can you feel what that child is feeling? It's time that parents stop murmuring about their children's problems and get hold of God for victory for them.

The very same thing often happens when you go to a brother or sister in the church for help. Many times the same thing happens when you go to a pastor, an elder or deacon, or a counselor of the church. They have no help to offer. All they can do is gossip about you to others. They don't help you. They destroy you. They can only murmur about what a bad person you are.

Often murmuring is a result of competition. Instead of helping one another and blessing one another, we are competing against each other. We murmur about anything and everything we can find in order to tear the other person down and make ourselves look bigger and better.

And Satan doesn't care who he uses. He often uses mature people who are supposed to know better. They do everything they can to smear the reputation of young people – who just might be the future leaders of the church and of society. It almost seems that they are saying, *"Let's get them!"*

Satan is delighted with this, for if the people of the church are occupied competing against one another and murmuring against one another, nothing good will happen there. God's power will not be manifested in that place. People may go through the routine of religion. They may have some lifeless programs. They may stay in the church for two hours. But when they go out the door, they will be empty.

That breaks God's heart. He loves the church.

> *Husbands, love your wives, even as Christ also loved the church, and gave himself for it;*
>
> Ephesians 5:25

With all of its problems, with all of its idiosyncrasies, Christ still loves the church. He gave Himself for the church. That is why Satan is so intent on destroying it. And one of the tools he uses most effectively to do it is murmuring.

The Church in Jerusalem was increasing. The people should have been happy. They should have been rejoicing. But some of them found cause to murmur.

In this case (thank God), the apostles had wisdom to deal with the problem. If we let Him, God will give us the solutions. He will lead us by the Spirit to victory. But murmuring, if not contained, will destroy us.

When murmuring gets into a church, the church quickly becomes lukewarm. It cannot be on fire for God and continue to murmur. I personally know some churches that are so cold that you could ice skate in the aisles. When a servant of God is invited to speak in those churches (someone with a burning message on his heart, someone who has waited on God in prayer and has heard from heaven), the response of the people is often negative.

"This is too much for me," they are thinking. *"We don't want that man* (or woman) *in our pulpit. Get him out of here!"*

Those churches wonder why they are not able to pay their bills. They wonder why they have so many problems. I don't wonder why. I know why. They are denying the most essential thing in the church — the power of the Holy Ghost. They have replaced the power with personal ambition, competition and murmuring; and the church has grown cold.

God doesn't want you to be lukewarm. Lukewarm people make Him sick. He said He would spew them out of His mouth:

> *So then because thou art lukewarm, and neither cold nor hot, I will spue thee out of my mouth.*
>
> Revelation 3:16

Even Satan doesn't like lukewarm people. If you are not totally committed to him, he is not happy with you either.

Many believers are one day here, the next day there. They are up one day, down the next. They are happy today, sad tomorrow. They go up and down more than a yoyo.

It is time to stand firm. You cannot serve two masters. Would you like it if your husband or wife had another lover? How would that make you feel?

The Bible is so clear on this issue:

> *No man can serve two masters: for either he will hate the one, and love the other; or else he will hold to the one, and despise the other. Ye cannot serve God and mammon.* Matthew 6:24

How do you suppose the two masters would feel? No doubt one of them would say, *"Look, you are taking advantage of me. I don't like this. You are not keeping your commitments. I can't let this continue."* The other master would feel the same way. And because you pleased neither master, you would be left hanging.

Then, when you are left hanging, Satan always appears to rescue you. He says:

> *"Now that I have taken you back, you must do everything that I want. You were rejected by everyone. You were left hanging, and I rescued you. Now you must obey me."*

At this point you may want to give Satan marching orders. You may say, *"Get out!"* But he will not be intimidated. *"It's too late for that," he will say. "You are in my control."* You may wonder how it happened. It probably started with murmuring. Lukewarmness is the result of murmuring.

Some preachers invite an evangelist to preach in their church. When he is gone, they begin to tear apart everything he preached and murmur against him to their people. Those men wonder why their ministry is not growing. I know why. Murmuring is not of God.

Israel's murmuring in the wilderness was remembered in New Testament times:

> *Neither MURMUR ye, as some of them also MURMURED, and were destroyed of the destroyer. Now all these things happened unto them for ensamples: and they are written for our admonition, upon whom the ends of the world are come. Wherefore let him that thinketh he standeth take heed lest he fall.* 1 Corinthians 10:10-12

God has good things in store for us. We must stand strong against the enemy. We must *"take heed"* and avoid murmuring. Since the day I came to understand the work of the enemy, I have purposed in my heart to keep on fulfilling God's will for my life – regardless of what happens. I intend to keep on sharing the love of God and teaching. I intend to keep on praying (in season and out). I intend to keep on giving myself totally to the Lord. I intend to keep on living by faith the way He wants me to live. I intend to keep on serving Him to the best of my ability. I will not murmur against God — whatever others do.

The Pharisees missed the blessing of God because they murmured at every little thing they could find wrong with Jesus and His disciples:

> *But their scribes and Pharisees MURMURED against his disciples, saying, Why do ye eat and drink with publicans and sinners?* Luke 5:30

> *And the Pharisees and scribes MURMURED, saying, This man receiveth sinners, and eateth with them.* Luke 15:2

> *And when they saw it, they all MURMURED, saying, That he was gone to be guest with a man that is a sinner.* Luke 19:7

Jesus forbid the disciples to murmur:

> *Jesus therefore answered and said unto them, MURMUR NOT among yourselves.* John 6:43

The only time the word *"murmur"* was used in the Book of Acts was the case of the Grecian widows. The Jerusalem Church grew and was blessed and prospered and reached out. It did not live out its life in murmuring.

Satan is clever. He knows that murmuring displeases God. He knows that murmuring brings lukewarmness.

So he does everything in his power to cause the saints to murmur.

One of the issues Satan used in Jerusalem to cause problems was race, the differences between the Grecians and the Hebrews. He is still using that tool effectively all over the world, especially in the advanced nations.

If I were Satan, I would convince church people that they can safely continue to live in their unspoken, underlying racism. No one will challenge them. The fact that they send missionaries to Africa, Asia and Latin America will more than cover up their true attitude towards other races. As long as they keep those unpopular sentiments hidden deep in their hearts, they will be okay.

After all, the third world needs our resources. Who else can they look to? As long as those resources flow, quiet bigotry will go unchallenged — for now.

I would cause them to forget that God is no respecter of persons.

> *For there is no respect of persons with God.*
>
> Romans 2:11

"What can be expected of mere mortals?" I would ask.

Another of the prime causes of murmuring and division in the Body of Christ is the fact that each believer has his own "pet doctrine." If I were Satan, I would make men believe that their particular pet doctrine is so important and world-changing that they must be willing to separate from all other brothers, if necessary, in order to maintain their doctrinal position. It so much easier to separate than to work out our differences. Working out our differences demands maturity. Working out our differences demands patience. Working out our differences demands sacrifice. *"Surely God would not expect those things of us,"* I would say.

What an ingenious deception! Learn to recognize what the Enemy of your soul is doing so that you can defeat him.

Chapter 10

IF I WERE SATAN:
I Would Do Everything Within My Power To Cause The Downfall Of Christian Leaders

And he gave some, apostles; and some, prophets; and some, evangelists; and some, pastors and teachers; For the perfecting of the saints, for the work of the ministry, for the edifying of the body of Christ: Till we all come in the unity of the faith, and of the knowledge of the Son of God, unto a perfect man, unto the measure of the stature of the fulness of Christ: Ephesians 4:11-13

If I were Satan, I would recognize the importance of Christian leaders. I would know that if I could make them stumble, many others would follow them. I would work very hard to that end. I would recognize that without a good pastor, the sheep will stray, and I would do everything I could to destroy the reputation of good pastors.

I would try to replace godly leaders with blind leaders of the blind:

> *And if the blind lead the blind, both shall fall into the ditch.* Matthew 15:14

I would place some of my own children in every congregation to act as hypocrites. So many people have their eyes on the hypocrites in the church. *"If every Christian is like that,"* they say, *"then I never want to serve God."*

Let me tell you something: If you hide behind a hypocrite, then you are smaller than a hypocrite. If somebody doesn't live right, you don't have to worry about it. Jesus will deal with that person. Your membership is not with man. Your membership is with God.

I have heard people say, *"I really want to do God's will. But do you remember that preacher that we had in here? All he talked about was money. I can't believe that was of God. That made me stumble."*

Satan will always have someone around to make you stumble — if you let him. He has a host of hypocrites and glory seekers that he can use — if you fall for it.

He knows that if you don't stumble over some hypocrite, you'll be strong to resist him. He knows that if you don't stumble over some of these pretenders, you will live victoriously over sin. He also knows that if he can con you into stumbling, it will have a domino effect. Someone else will see you stumble and say, "*See that! I knew that person was a hypocrite all along. That's the reason I don't go to church. That's the reason I don't do the will of God. Did you hear him say last week that he loved God? Now look at him. What a hypocrite!*"

If I were Satan, I would tell people, "*You shouldn't believe anything evangelists say. There are so many bad ones. You never know who is sincere and who isn't. You can't trust them. They all have one thing in common. They are all a bunch of thieves. They are nothing but crooks. Everyone knows that.*"

There may be some insincere evangelists. Some of them may be crooks. But I don't have to worry about that. Their dishonesty will catch up with them. God will take care of them. I won't let the existence of hypocrites and insincere people hinder me.

Some people still look to hypocrites they knew as small children. "*I remember as a little girl,*" they say. "*I remember as a little boy, when I was growing up, the preacher in our church did something that really hurt me. From that time on I have kept my distance from the church. I can never again give my self unreservedly to religion.*"

That man will give an account of his deeds. If he was God's true servant, God dealt with him. If he was Satan's servant, he got his pay as well. Don't worry about him. Put him out of your mind. Don't stumble because of something a man did. God is not a man, and you can trust Him.

> *God is not a man, that he should lie; neither the son of man, that he should repent: hath he said, and shall he not do it? or hath he spoken, and shall he not make it good?* Numbers 23:19

> *God is faithful, by whom ye were called unto the fellowship of his Son Jesus Christ our Lord.*
> 1 Corinthians 1:9

Serve God. He will never hurt you. He will never let you down. He will never take advantage of you. He loves you and is waiting for you with open arms.

Don't worry about hypocrites. If Satan has caused you to stumble because of something some hypocritical person did, I hope you can see how foolish that is. Rise above that and take the victory God has prepared for you.

If I were Satan, I would try to convince people that the failure of others is all God's fault. I would tell them not to blame people. I would convince them that God fails people sometimes, that He is not reliable, not to be trusted. I would tell them that sometimes He is very slow to act in defense of His own. *"Don't put much trust in God,"* I would say. *"Use your own head. Use some common sense."*

I would cause men to ignore the assurances of Scripture:

> *For God is not unrighteous to forget your work and labour of love, which ye have shewed toward his name ... .*
> Hebrews 6:10

> *The Lord is not slack concerning his promise ... .*
> 2 Peter 3:9

I would sow confusion in the Church to destroy its power. I would sow a lack of confidence in one another. I would sow suspicion. I would sow discord.

Satan does it well, for he is the author of confusion:

> *For God is not the author of confusion, but of peace, as in all churches of the saints.*
> 1 Corinthians 14:33

If I were Satan, I would attack Christian leadership with all my strength. When a prominent leader fell in any way, I would rejoice and cause others to rejoice. I would print it in every newspaper and keep people talking about it by bringing it up again from time to time.

I would cause people to scrutinize ministers so carefully and with such mistrust that they would misunderstand their words and actions and would libel them with accusations of financial and sexual misconduct. I would cause people to mistake the anointing for arrogance and a desire to control other people. I would have others read sexual undertones into the normal expression of God's love in His servants. If I could convince the Board to remove them from office, I would do it.

We must join forces to resist these insidious attacks of Satan. He may be a master at deceit, but he is no match for the power of our God. We are more than conquerors through Christ. Rise us, saints of God. Put Satan in his place.

Chapter 11

IF I WERE SATAN:
I Would Inspire Preachers and Teachers To Present Another Gospel

But though we, or an angel from heaven, preach any other gospel unto you than that which we have preached unto you, let him be accursed.

Galatians 1:8

If I were Satan, I would try to make people forget the true Gospel by giving them another gospel. Satan doesn't care if we are religious. He doesn't care if we attend church often. He is only concerned that we don't obey the true Gospel. He inspires preachers to say:

> *"God is so good that He would not make anyone go to hell – regardless of what they believe or the way they live. I can't believe that a good Lord would do that to His children. God will not do evil to anybody. God is so good that He will let everyone go to heaven."*

Satan would have us to ignore the true Gospel:

> *For he that soweth to his flesh shall of the flesh reap corruption; but he that soweth to the Spirit shall of the Spirit reap life everlasting.* Galatians 6:8

God doesn't send people to hell. Contrary to Satan's lies, people send themselves to hell. Don't believe another gospel.

Satan would love for preachers to ignore the most important aspects of the Word of God and concentrate on a social gospel. He tells men that the most important topic of the day is world peace, a new world order. They should concentrate on it and preach it. If I were Satan, I would involve preachers in political activity to promote these lofty goals. That would keep them so busy they wouldn't have time to do God's work.

I would tell preachers how important it is to feed people. I would make sure they spend most of their time concerned with the food supply. If they try to feed all the people Satan keeps in poverty, that would keep them so busy they wouldn't have time to preach repentance and deliverance through the blood of Jesus. A gospel that doesn't have power to deliver through the blood of Jesus is not of God. It is another gospel.

I would tell Christian leaders that they should just concentrate on education. I would lie to them and tell them, *"If people were better educated, they would serve God."* I would make sure that all their time is taken up with education so that they don't have time to preach the truth.

I would encourage preachers to fill their sermons with current events, book reviews, and plenty of jokes to keep the sophisticated, the intellectual, and the unspiritual people entertained and interested. Since people are not willing to sit long in the church anyway, that wouldn't leave preachers much time to tell the truth.

I would have preachers tell people that it wasn't really necessary to make a public show of receiving Jesus into their hearts. *"Just be a good mate,"* I would have them preach. *"That is all God requires of you. Just love your family. Just love your neighbors. If you are loving and go to church sometimes, you will make it to heaven."*

These are common lies of our Enemy. The Bible declares:

> *Whosoever therefore shall confess me before men, him will I confess also before my Father which is in heaven.* Matthew 10:32

But Satan has his own agenda, and many are following him.

If I were Satan, I would cause preachers to put forth as examples of true Christianity people who are morally good, but have made little commitment to God. I would use famous people as much as possible, even Hollywood stars. That would assure a good audience, and people would be deceived into believing that the lifestyle of all famous people is acceptable.

I would use as examples of the Christian life people who don't even go to church and would try to say that they are better than many people who do attend regularly.

> *"They don't drink. They don't smoke. They don't curse. The good Lord knows they love their neighbors and do many good deeds. They are excellent role models."*

I would promote such people for office in the church. In this way, I would be telling everyone that all you need to do to go to heaven is be kind and good.

I want to declare to you through the pages of this book that you can love your neighbors and do good deeds and still go to hell – if you don't love Jesus and do His will. Stop believing the lies of Satan. God is still a holy God, and He is still looking for a holy people. Wake up to the tactics that Satan has mastered so well.

If I were Satan, I would slowly, but surely, eliminate the word *"holiness"* from the vocabulary of preachers. After all, the mention of holiness in offensive to many people, and the word has been abused and misused. I would cause people to forget what God said:

> *Having therefore these promises, dearly beloved, let us cleanse ourselves from all filthiness of the flesh and spirit, perfecting HOLINESS in the fear of God.* 2 Corinthians 7:1

> *Follow peace with all men, and HOLINESS, without which no man shall see the Lord:*
> Hebrews 12:14

Since Satan doesn't want people to *"see the Lord,"* he certainly doesn't want them to live a holy life. Now we are told it is impossible to live a holy life, so most people have stopped trying to live right. *"God doesn't even expect it,"* is the new gospel being presented.

But God hasn't changed. His will hasn't changed. His Word hasn't changed. And the truth of the Gospel has not changed. Reject Satan's lies and live victoriously in Jesus Christ.

Chapter 12

IF I WERE SATAN:
I Would Do Anything To Keep Christians From Making A Commitment To God and the Church

Some trust in chariots, and some in horses: but we will remember the name of the Lord our God.

Psalms 20:7

If I were Satan, I would confuse commitment to a particular denomination with a commitment to God and THE CHURCH. Some people say:

> *"I was born a Baptist, thank God, and I am going to die a Baptist."* (Put in your own particular denomination.)

I think those people are already dead. No church is a refuge. Only Jesus Christ can save. He is the Way, the Truth, and the Life. And no one comes to the Father but by Him. He said it Himself (John 14:6).

You won't find a church that can save people. Salvation is only by grace and through faith in Jesus Christ. Stop believing Satan's lies.

If I were Satan, I would cause people to ignore the Bible truth of how to be saved:

> *For by grace are ye saved through faith; and that not of yourselves: it is the gift of God:*
>
> Ephesians 2:8

I would tell people that they can be saved by their good works. I would convince them that they had much to boast about, reminding them often of the good things they have done:

> *"You always treat your neighbor right. You are a good person, and the Lord knows your heart. The good Lord knows that you're sincere. He remembers that you go to church once every year without fail, and He knows that you have supported the missionary programs of the church."*

Men love to boast, and Satan loves it when they do. God said:

Not of works, lest any man should boast.

Ephesians 2:9

When men feel that they have something to boast about, they become unconcerned about a commitment to God. They don't understand why that is necessary. They feel that they are good enough. Satan continually assures them that they are right. Jesus shows us the error of that kind of thinking:

> *And when he was gone forth into the way, there came one running, and kneeled to him, and asked him, Good Master, what shall I do that I may inherit eternal life? And Jesus said unto him, Why callest thou me good? there is none good but one, that is, God. Thou knowest the commandments, Do not commit adultery, Do not kill, Do not steal, Do not bear false witness, Defraud not, Honour thy father and mother. And he answered and said unto him, Master, all these have I observed from my youth. Then Jesus beholding him loved him, and said unto him, One thing thou lackest: go thy way, sell whatsoever thou hast, and give to the poor, and thou shalt have treasure in heaven: and come, take up the cross, and follow me. And he was sad at that saying, and went away grieved: for he had great possessions.*
>
> Mark 10:17-22

When we read about this young man coming to Jesus, we can sense the sincerity of his desire to have "*everlasting life.*" That day, when Jesus mentioned the commandments, the surprising reply was *"all these have I observed from my youth."* He had done it all. He was a good man. Most people would have considered him to be exemplary. But Jesus told him he was lacking something. He needed to make a full commitment to God. He needed to show that he loved God more than anything else. He needed to take up his cross and follow Jesus wholly. That thought made the man sad — *"for he had great possessions."*

Satan will use anything at all to keep you from making a full commitment to God. Here in North America and in Europe he has the perfect tool. The fear of having to give up their riches keeps many from taking up the cross and following Jesus. What He said to the disciples that day should shake every American, Canadian and European into making a full commitment to God.

> *And Jesus looked round about, and saith unto his disciples, How hardly shall they that have riches enter into the kingdom of God! And the disciples were astonished at his words. But Jesus answereth again, and saith unto them, Children, how hard is it for them that trust in riches to enter into the kingdom of God! It is easier for a camel to go through the eye of a needle, than for a rich man to enter into the kingdom of God. And they were astonished out of measure, saying among themselves, Who then can be saved? And Jesus looking upon them saith, With men it is impossible, but not with God: for with God all things are possible.* Mark 10:23-27

Riches and the lust for riches can easily keep you out of heaven. God is demanding commitment of those who will enter those gates and live with Him forever. He is not accepting any excuses. It is all or nothing.

If I were Satan, I would use pride to keep believers from making a full commitment to God. Satan understands pride. It was pride that robbed him of his destiny. He is a master at using the technique on others.

If men have money, Satan tries to make them feel proud. Many actually feel that as long as they have money, they don't need God.

If women are beautiful, Satan tries to make them vain. Many of them actually feel that as long as they have a physical attractiveness they have no need of God.

When young people get a little education, Satan uses that to cause them to be proud and to forget God. The educational system contributes to this pride by blocking out the knowledge that everything came from God and that nothing could exist without His Word. Many young people begin to feel that they don't need God and the church.

Pride is a terrible thing. It is so destructive. It is rebellion against God, and He cannot tolerate it. He hates pride.

> *PRIDE, and arrogancy, and the evil way, and the froward mouth, do I hate.* Proverbs 8:13

Proud people are headed for a fall.

> *PRIDE goeth before destruction, and AN HAUGHTY SPIRIT before a fall.*
>
> Proverbs 16:18

There is altogether too much pride in the church. Satan loves it, but God hates it. Satan rewards it, but God punishes it.

Some people are too proud to go to the altar and confess their sins. They would rather maintain their *"pride"* than know the forgiveness of sins through Jesus Christ.

Some people are too proud to get prayed for when they are sick or in trouble. They would rather maintain their *"pride"* and go on suffering.

Some people are too proud to seek the Holy Ghost. They would rather maintain their *"pride"* and go on living powerless lives.

Some people are too proud to receive money from others. They would rather maintain their *"pride"* and go on in deprivation and need. Pride is a terrible thing. God hates it!

Pride is so foolish. What do we have to be so proud of? What does it hurt us to admit our need? Is everyone else perfect except you? Think about it. Yet Satan uses this insidious sin to keep people from making a complete commitment to God.

Those Christians who are reluctant to make a commitment to God are cannot experience His blessings and divine protection. Don't be deceived by the enemy's lies. Total commitment is necessary. Jesus must be Lord of your life. Church cannot be a convenient part of your social life. God wants to rule your heart. If He cannot, then you cannot be part of His Kingdom. You can't put God off anytime you feel like it. You must make Him Lord of all — at all times.

Satan's deception has kept millions out of the Kingdom.

If I were Satan, I would do everything possible to stop believers from supporting the work of the Lord through their generous offerings. I would make the word "tithe" (which means the tenth of our income that belongs to God) a foreign word to many church people. I would give them every reason not to tithe, and would cause them to totally ignore the Word of God, which says:

> *Will a man rob God? Yet ye have robbed me. But ye say, Wherein have we robbed thee? In tithes and offerings. Ye are cursed with a curse: for ye have robbed me, even this whole nation. Bring ye all the tithes into the storehouse, that there may be meat in mine house, and prove me now herewith, saith the Lord of hosts, if I will not open you the windows of heaven, and pour you out a blessing, that there shall not be room enough to receive it.*
>
> Malachi 3:8-10

I would help people to justify their theft, knowing that in robbing God they would be robbing themselves and robbing the church. I would make them want all the blessings of the Christian life without accepting any of the responsibilities.

Not only would I make every effort to keep Christians from having a generous spirit. I would also try to convince them not to be so hospitable. *"That's old fashioned,"* I would say. *"Nobody expects that of you any more."* I would make them forget what the Bible teaches:

> *Distributing to the necessity of saints; given to HOSPITALITY.* Romans 12:13

> *A bishop then must be blameless, the husband of one wife, vigilant, sober, of good behaviour, given to HOSPITALITY, apt to teach;*
> 1 Timothy 3:2

> *Be not forgetful to entertain strangers: for thereby some have entertained angels unawares.*
> Hebrews 13:2

> *Use HOSPITALITY one to another without grudging.* 1 Peter 4:9

If I were Satan, I would do exactly what he is doing.

Chapter 13

IF I WERE SATAN:
I Would Glorify Poverty

> *Beloved, I wish above all things that thou mayest prosper and be in health, even as thy soul prospereth.* 3 John 1:2

If I were Satan, I would make poverty and lack synonymous with holiness and goodness. I would make people believe that owning anything is not spiritual, that having money is not consistent with holiness, and that investments or savings are a sign of carnality. I would actually convince people that money in any form is an unnecessary evil. I would cause them to misquote the Scriptures:

> *For the love of money is the root of all evil:*
> 1 Timothy 6:10

Instead of knowing that *"the love of money is the root of all evil,"* I would have them believe that money itself is the root of all evil.

I would convince churches that it is not necessary to conduct their affairs in a businesslike manner. I would ridicule time management and the thought of financial security. In this way I would make Christian into *"unprofitable"* servants.

> *And so he that had received five talents came and brought other five talents, saying, Lord, thou deliveredst unto me five talents: behold, I have gained beside them five talents more. His lord said unto him, Well done, thou good and faithful servant: thou hast been faithful over a few things, I will make thee ruler over many things: enter thou into the joy of thy lord.*
> *He also that had received two talents came and said, Lord, thou deliveredst unto me two talents: behold, I have gained two other talents beside them. His lord said unto him, Well done, good and faithful servant; thou hast been faithful over a few things, I will make thee ruler over many things: enter thou into the joy of thy lord.*
> *Then he which had received the one talent came and said, Lord, I knew thee that thou art an hard*

man, reaping where thou hast not sown, and gathering where thou hast not strawed: And I was afraid, and went and hid thy talent in the earth: lo, there thou hast that is thine. His lord answered and said unto him, Thou wicked and slothful servant, thou knewest that I reap where I sowed not, and gather where I have not strawed: Thou oughtest therefore to have put my money to the exchangers, and then at my coming I should have received mine own with usury. Take therefore the talent from him, and give it unto him which hath ten talents. For unto every one that hath shall be given, and he shall have abundance: but from him that hath not shall be taken away even that which he hath. And cast ye the unprofitable servant into outer darkness: there shall be weeping and gnashing of teeth.

Matthew 25:20-30

Poor management doesn't get any praise from God, and it certainly doesn't glorify Him.

To further my ends, I would consider the church the best place to produce lazy, sloppy, and untidy people. I would especially target Pentecostal churches.

In order to keep Christians poor, I would prevent them from getting the best jobs. To accomplish that I would convince Christians not to give their very best when they go to work. I would make sure they use their bosses time to pray and read the Bible. I would make them very critical of their "unsaved" bosses so that they would be uncooperative and hard to get along with on the job.

I would do everything to make them go to work late and be the first to leave the office in the afternoon. I would give them every opportunity to call in sick to keep from going to work at all. In short, I would make them unreliable employees. In this way I would be accomplishing three things. **1)** I would be keeping Christians and the Church poor, and **2)** I would be destroying the testimony of the believers and **3)** keeping many more people from accepting the faith.

I would make it a point to see that Christians are kept from buying houses. I would tell them that it was better not to own anything because Jesus is coming soon and that they need to keep their suitcases packed and ready for the next flight to heaven.

I would convince Christians not to pay their bills on time — even if they do have the money. In this way I could cause them to have a bad credit rating so that banks would have no confidence in churches or their members.

I would cause Christians to be so "spiritual" that they write would bad checks "by faith" to the church and that a good percentage of the income of the church would come back in bounced checks.

I would teach Christians to depend more and more on the government for their income. The government is not going to print Bibles. Only the Church will print Bibles. The government will not send missionaries. Only the Church can send missionaries. The government will not build churches. Only the Church will build other churches.

Do you see why Satan wants to keep you poor? He doesn't want you to have a good testimony. He doesn't want the church to be able to do its work properly. He doesn't want you to be able to reach out to the whole world.

God wants you to prosper so that you can give more for the spread of the Gospel. Satan is determined to keep you poor. He will do anything to prevent the expansion of the Kingdom to other nations.

There is no way to get to Africa, Asia or Latin America without a ticket for an airplane or a boat. God's servants need sturdy and reliable vehicles to travel within national borders and gasoline and spare parts for those vehicles. It takes money to buy all these things.

If you don't believe it takes money to live the Christian life, go to a Christian bookstore, pick out a nice Bible, and try to take it without paying for it.

Go to the gasoline station. Tell them you are a servant of God and see if they fill your tank for free.

Don't pay your rent one month and see what your landlord does.

The next time you get a speeding ticket, just pray over it instead of paying the fine.

You will soon find out that money is an essential part of the Christian life. God wants you to have money. Satan wants to keep you poor.

The thing I don't understand is why poverty is so attractive to many people. Being poor is nothing to brag about. Being poor is nothing to be happy about.

Satan is the author of poverty. God is the author of prosperity.

Take God at His word. Resist the lies of the Enemy, and move into God's prosperity so that you can be a part of the furtherance of the Gospel in these last days.

Chapter 14

IF I WERE SATAN:
I Would Keep Men From Fulfilling Their God-Given Responsibilities

(For if a man know not how to rule his own house, how shall he take care of the church of God?)
1 Timothy 3:5

If I were Satan, I would work especially hard on men. After all, I wouldn't want them to realize their true potential, and I certainly wouldn't want them to lead their families into the blessings of God.

I would convince some men to become totally consumed with their work. I would make them hopeless workaholics. I would make sure they are too busy to be part of the development of their children or to show interest in family interaction or growth.

I would cause men to love the golf course and the tennis course more than they love the House of God. I would interest men in antique cars, model airplanes, architectural designs — anything to keep them from family and church responsibilities.

I would make men love electronic gadgets and the remote control of the television set more than they love the Bible.

I would convince men that religion is only for the weak, the defeated, the oppressed and children. I would make it difficult for them to pray for more than a few minutes at a time.

I would make men think that it was a worthy thing to relinquish their position as spiritual head of the family to their wives. I would be delighted when men neglected these responsibilities and women had to step in and take them over.

I would convince men that showing their emotions is a sign of weakness and that they should have a superficial relationship with their family, their God and their fellow believers. I would make them react very offensively when confronted.

I would make men feel justified in staying home and sending the family to church. Many men expect their wives to be religious, to be committed to the church, and to participate in its activities. At the same time, they are not religious, are not committed to the church, and do not participate in its activities.

I would cause the mind of man to dwell more on the lyrics of every sensual record and latest hit song rather than on the hymns of our fathers.

I could cause man's loyalty to his national political leaders to be replaced by criticism and insult. God says:

> *I exhort therefore, that, first of all, supplications, prayers, intercessions, and giving of thanks, be made for all men; For kings, and FOR ALL THAT ARE IN AUTHORITY; that we may lead a quiet and peaceable life in all godliness and honesty. For this is good and acceptable in the sight of God our Saviour;* 1 Timothy 2:1-3

Because I was born in a third-world nation, I have a great appreciation of America as a nation. Even though I have traveled extensively in Europe I can say that no nation compares to the greatness of America. Yet I have noticed that many Americans take their liberty for granted. Instead of being grateful for their freedom, they seek excessive independence which results in criticism and disobedience to the authority of their elected and appointed officials.

Many are blinded to all the good in America and can only see the bad.

Men, let's rise up and cast off the works of darkness. God has a great destiny for every one of us. Take your rightful place in the Church and the community. Don't let Satan steal God's best from you any longer.

Chapter 15

IF I WERE SATAN:
I Would Cause Those Who Have Prospered to Feel At Ease

> *Thou sayest, I am rich, and increased with goods, and have need of nothing; and knowest not that thou art wretched, and miserable, and poor, and blind, and naked:* Revelation 3:17

If I were Satan, I would do everything in my power to cause those who have prospered to be at ease. I would use the fall of the Berlin Wall and the collapse of communism throughout Eastern Europe to convince the church that she has triumphed at last, and can now rest. I would make Christians feel just as satisfied as the man whom Jesus described in His parable:

> *And he spake a parable unto them, saying, The ground of a certain rich man brought forth plentifully: And he thought within himself, saying, What shall I do, because I have no room where to bestow my fruits? And he said, This will I do: I will pull down my barns, and build greater; and there will I bestow all my fruits and my goods. And I will say to my soul, Soul, thou hast much goods laid up for many years;* TAKE THINE EASE, *eat, drink, and be merry. But God said unto him, Thou fool, this night thy soul shall be required of thee: then whose shall those things be, which thou hast provided? So is he that layeth up treasure for himself, and is not rich toward God.*
>
> Luke 12:17-21

I would make the church believe that all her missions over the years have earned her a special place in the heart of God, so that her ticket to Heaven is assured. She can relax now, be at ease, and enjoy her prosperity. She has nothing to be concerned about. She can stop worrying about world evangelism and start indulging herself more.

I would make her believe she is truly God's gift to the world. I would instill a sense that her priorities supersede the needs of the poor, the widow, and the orphan. They are more critical than that of the drug addict or the prostitute.

If I were Satan, I would occupy the church with beautifying herself constantly rather than using her resources for spreading the Gospel. I would instill in her an obsession with appearance, causing her to spend more time and money primping than on anything else.

I would do everything in my power to cause the church to waste time, money and resources on dead-end causes. I would constantly point out the wrong problem and would raise up my own servants in her midst to give false direction to this end. I would cause the men of the church to be so caught up with their own wants and desires and visions and plans that they could not even see the needs of their own spouses and children.

I would make the church in North America believe that its particular brand of Christianity is so far superior to others that it is actually *"the apple of God's eye."* I would encourage her to continue to export a mix of faith in God and Western culture, so that the little *"Western culture centers"* she would be opening in many places would have little resemblance to the true Church of the Lord Jesus Christ. Thinking that she was planting churches, she would be planting confusion among the peoples of the so-called third-world countries.

I would delude Christians into believing that God owes them for all their hard work and sacrifice. I wouldn't mind if the church were rich — as long as all the money is spent for the wrong things. That would play into my hands. I could then convince her that she had need of nothing, not even God.

I would teach rich Christians to hoard the wealth that God gave them, assuring them that God did not bless them with prosperity to win the world, but that the prosperity came because the world owed it to them for their goodness. *"Now,"* I would tell them, *"it is time to 'kick back' and enjoy life. You deserve it. You earned it. You are worth it. You deserve the very best."* And I would lull them to sleep.

I would cause them to ignore the Old Testament admonition:

> *And it shall be, when the Lord thy God shall have brought thee into the land which he sware unto thy fathers, to Abraham, to Isaac, and to Jacob, to give thee great and goodly cities, which thou buildedst not, And houses full of all good things, which thou filledst not, and wells digged, which thou diggedst not, vineyards and olive trees, which thou plantedst not; when thou shalt have eaten and be full; Then BEWARE LEST THOU FORGET THE LORD, which brought thee forth out of the land of Egypt, from the house of bondage.*
>
> Deuteronomy 6:10-12

I am sure you can agree that Satan has already mastered these tactics well. If you have been entrapped by them, it is time to rise up and cast off the chains of bondage. Be free in the Lord Jesus.

Chapter 16

IF I WERE SATAN:
I Would Disguise the Real Harvest

Say not ye, There are yet four months, and then cometh harvest? behold, I say unto you, Lift up your eyes, and look on the fields; for they are white already to harvest. John 4:35

If I were Satan, I would disguise the greatest harvest that God ever prepared. I would cause even the elect of God to be fooled into believing that those who are hungry for truth are actually dangerous false religionists. Instead of embracing them and winning them, they should drive them away.

This is what I believe has happened with those who are members of what we now call *"the New Age Movement."* The church fasted, prayed and believed God for many years for a harvest. Then, when fifty million people began searching in Eastern religions and mysticism, instead of the church rising up in the power of the Holy Spirit and ministering the true Gospel to these hungry people, the church leaders panicked and proclaimed these people to be our worst enemies. I believe the majority of these people presented little threat to Christianity, but were only intellectually searching for truth. I doubt the theory of the great conspiracy to pull people from their churches and damn their souls. If our people are well grounded in the Lord, nothing can pull them away.

> *My sheep hear my voice, and I know them, and they follow me:* John 10:27

The purpose of Satan in all this is not only to disguise the harvest and pit us against the thirsty souls of our time, but also to keep us occupied while the true enemy of Christianity takes up his position against us. For while we are thus occupied, a well planned, well-financed assault is being made against us, and most of us don't even recognize it.

Our real enemy today is not the New Age Movement, but a militant Islam. While we sit back, these militant Islamic forces take control of whole sectors of our economy and of our youth. While we wrestle with phantoms, Islam assaults the culture of black America and sections of the African continent in an unprecedented way. As they have in other generations, militant Islamic forces are massing on every continent for an assault to destroy the church through a holy war and to rule large portions of the earth. The present events in the Middle East are not just window dressing. This is a real battle (See Jeremiah 50 and 51).

At some point, the church will wake up and realize what is happening, but that may very well be too late. The harvest may, by then, be lost; and the enemy may be fully entrenched.

Satan is a master deceiver. Wake up, Church, before it is too late. Use your God-given wealth to reach out to the nations quickly, while there is time.

Part III

Your Weapons and Your Decision

Chapter 17

Your Weapons Against Satan

If God be for us, who can be against us?
Romans 8:31

Satan is a master deceiver. He is clever. He is good at his work. But you don't have to be one of his victims. His power is nothing compared to God's power. The Scriptures declare that God is for us and that because it is so, no one else can prosper against us. With God on our side, we can conquer every foe. No demon can harm us. The Devil himself will have to flee from our presence. But it doesn't just happen. There are some definite steps that you must take.

Once you have learned to recognize the work of the enemy, once you know him and his tactics, then you must arm yourself against him. You cannot wait until some moment of crisis. When Satan attacks, it is too late to prepare. You must prepare now. God has provided armor for you; put it on. God has provided weapons for you; learn to use them.

First put on your defensive armor. Gird your loins with truth. Put on the breastplate of righteousness. Get your feet shod with the *"preparation of the gospel of peace."* Pick up *"the shield of faith."*

When you get your armor in place, begin to pick up some of your spiritual weapons:

1. Obedience

Obedience may not sound like a weapon to you, but it is. When you submit yourself to God, He builds a protective hedge around you that protects you from the onslaught of the Enemy.

> *Submit yourselves therefore to God. Resist the devil, and he will flee from you.* James 4:7

If your life is not submitted to the will of God, no weapon will work properly for you. It is God's power in you that makes every weapon effective.

Secondly, when you submit to those who are placed by God in leadership over you, they *"watch for your souls."*

> *Obey them that have the rule over you, and submit yourselves: for they watch for your souls, as they that must give account, that they may do it with joy, and not with grief: for that is unprofitable for you.*
> Hebrews 13:17

A child is defenseless in this world, but when that child is under the protection of a loving mother or father, no harm will come to him. No enemy has a chance against protective parents.

A tiny bird, newly hatched from the egg, is totally defenseless. But if that tiny bird will stay in the nest, under the protection of the mother bird or father bird, no harm will come to it. Commitment brings you under the protection of God and of His servants.

Living a life of obedience and submission to God involves knowing His will for your life and doing His will. He may make that will known to your personally, or He may reveal His will to you through your pastors and mature leaders. Don't be rebellious to what He is showing you either way. When you wander away from the Body, you become an easy prey for the wolves of this world. Submit yourself for your own protection.

2. The Word of God

When Paul wrote to the Ephesians about putting on "*the whole armour,*" the first weapon he mentioned (apart from the pieces of armor) was "*the sword of the Spirit – which is the word of God.*" No weapon could be more important than the Word of God. The Bible is a powerful tool that God has given to us. Learn to use it wisely.

We have always depended on the preachers to open the Word of God and tell us God's will for our lives. But we are now living in a different day. God has blessed so many of us with the ability to read and has placed the Word of God in our hands. We are now responsible before God as individuals. He expects us to go to the Book and find the truth for ourselves. He expects us to learn His ways for ourselves. He expects us to arm ourselves. Get your weapons ready. Don't dare face the enemy unarmed.

Read the Word of God for yourself. If God could teach Peter, an uneducated fisherman, He can surely teach you. Don't blame preachers for what may or may not tell you. The time has come for you to hear God for yourself. The time has come for you to know what the Word of God says. God loves you and wants to make His Word real to you. Do your part.

3. The Blood of Jesus

The blood of Jesus is a powerful weapon against Satan. First, you must be sure that you are redeemed by His blood. If you have never been covered by the blood of Jesus, you are vulnerable and defenseless against the Enemy.

> *Much more then, being now justified BY HIS BLOOD, we shall be saved from wrath through him.* Romans 5:9

> *In whom we have redemption THROUGH HIS BLOOD, the forgiveness of sins, according to the riches of his grace;* Ephesians 1:7

The blood of Jesus is the New Testament covenant, replacing the animal sacrifices of the Old.

> *Likewise also the cup after supper, saying, This cup is the new testament in my blood, which is shed for you.* Luke 22:20

> *After the same manner also he took the cup, when he had supped, saying, This cup is the new testament in my blood: this do ye, as oft as ye drink it, in remembrance of me.* 1 Corinthians 11:25

This involves more than partaking of the communion table. It involves partaking of Jesus:

> *Then Jesus said unto them, Verily, verily, I say unto you, Except ye eat the flesh of the Son of man, and drink his blood, ye have no life in you. Whoso eateth my flesh, and drinketh my blood, hath eternal life; and I will raise him up at the last day. For my flesh is meat indeed, and my blood is drink indeed. He that eateth my flesh, and drinketh my blood, dwelleth in me, and I in him.* John 6:53-56

It involves having *"faith in His blood."*

> *Whom God hath set forth to be a propitiation THROUGH FAITH IN HIS BLOOD, to declare*

his righteousness for the remission of sins that are past, through the forbearance of God;

Romans 3:25

Faith in the working of the blood of Jesus in our lives gives us a boldness before the throne of God and in the face of the Enemy, as well.

Having therefore, brethren, boldness to enter into the holiest BY THE BLOOD OF JESUS,

Hebrews 10:19

And they overcame him by the blood of the Lamb, and by the word of their testimony.

Revelation 12:11

Just as the death angel passed over the houses where the blood had been applied in Egypt, so the Devil is powerless against us when we have the blood of Jesus applied to our hearts.

The work of redemption by the blood of Jesus may be a one-time thing, but there is a need for the constant renewal of the application of the blood of Jesus in our lives.

But if we walk in the light, as he is in the light, we have fellowship one with another, and the blood of Jesus Christ his Son cleanseth us from all sin.

1 John 1:7

Don't neglect this powerful weapon. Use it well.

4. The Name of Jesus

Devils tremble when the name of Jesus is mentioned. They believe in Him and fear Him.

> *Thou believest that there is one God; thou doest well: the devils also believe, and tremble.*
>
> James 2:19

There are many ways to use the name of Jesus as an effective weapon. Here are a few of them:

Learn to pray in the name of Jesus.

> *And whatsoever ye shall ask IN MY NAME, that will I do, that the Father may be glorified in the Son. If ye shall ask any thing IN MY NAME, I will do it.*
>
> John 14:13-14

> *Verily, verily, I say unto you, Whatsoever ye shall ask the Father IN MY NAME, he will give it you. Hitherto have ye asked nothing IN MY NAME: ask, and ye shall receive, that your joy may be full.*
>
> John 16:23-24

Deal with demons in the name of Jesus.

> *And these signs shall follow them that believe; In MY NAME shall they cast out devils;*
>
> Mark 16:17

Paul, being grieved, turned and said to the spirit, I command thee IN THE NAME OF JESUS CHRIST to come out of her. And he came out the same hour. Acts 16:18

Minister healing in the name of Jesus.

Then Peter said, Silver and gold have I none; but such as I have give I thee: IN THE NAME OF JESUS CHRIST OF NAZARETH rise up and walk. Acts 3:6

And HIS NAME through faith in HIS NAME hath made this man strong, whom ye see and know: yea, the faith which is by him hath given him this perfect soundness in the presence of you all. Acts 3:16

Be it known unto you all, and to all the people of Israel, that BY THE NAME OF JESUS CHRIST OF NAZARETH, whom ye crucified, whom God raised from the dead, even by him doth this man stand here before you whole. Acts 4:10

Preach in the name of Jesus.

And that repentance and remission of sins should be preached IN HIS NAME among all nations, beginning at Jerusalem. Luke 24:47

But Barnabas took him, and brought him to the apostles, and declared unto them how he had seen the Lord in the way, and that he had spoken to him, and how he had preached boldly at Damascus IN THE NAME OF JESUS. Acts 9:27

And he spake boldly IN THE NAME OF THE LORD JESUS. Acts 9:29

Even give thanks in the name of Jesus.

Giving thanks always for all things unto God and the Father IN THE NAME OF OUR LORD JESUS CHRIST; Ephesians 5:20

His name is holy.

And he said unto them, When ye pray, say, Our Father which art in heaven, HALLOWED BY THY NAME. Thy kingdom come. Thy will be done, as in heaven, so in earth. Luke 11:2

His name is above "*every name that is named.*"

FAR ABOVE all principality, and power, and might, and dominion, and EVERY NAME THAT IS NAMED, not only in this world, but also in that which is to come: Ephesians 1:21

Wherefore God also hath highly exalted him, and given him A NAME WHICH IS ABOVE EVERY NAME: That at the name of Jesus every knee should bow, of things in heaven, and things in earth, and things under the earth; And that every

tongue should confess that Jesus Christ is Lord, to the glory of God the Father.
Philippians 2:9-11

The enemies of the Gospel feared the name of Jesus. They commanded the disciples not to use that name anymore.

And they called them, and commanded them not to speak at all nor teach IN THE NAME OF JESUS. Acts 4:18

When the disciples did not obey, the religious leaders were angry:

Did not we straitly command you that ye should not teach IN THIS NAME? and, behold, ye have filled Jerusalem with your doctrine, and intend to bring this man's blood upon us. Acts 5:28

Again they commanded that this powerful name not be invoked.

And when they had called the apostles, and beaten them, they commanded that they should not speak IN THE NAME OF JESUS, and let them go.
Acts 5:40

But the first-century disciples could not be silenced. They had learned to use the name of Jesus as an effective weapon and were not about to give it up. That name brought them victory over every enemy. It will do the same for you.

5. Personal Testimony

And they overcame him by the blood of the Lamb, and by the word of their testimony.
Revelation 12:11

Your personal testimony is one of your most powerful weapons. Protect it. The fact that the Lord redeemed you from a past life of sin, changed your life totally and set you on the path of righteousness should cause every demon to fear.

When the Devil approaches you, remind him of the grace of God in your life. Remind him of the pit you came from. Remind him of God's love for you.

If your testimony is weak, Satan will remind you of that fact every time you get on your knees to pray. If you are one of those inconsistent Christians, Satan will use it against you every time. Don't give him the chance. Guard your testimony and use it effectively against him.

6. The Power of the Holy Ghost

Learn to use the power of God and the authority of God that is in you by the Holy Ghost. Jesus said to the devil:

Get thee behind me, Satan: Matthew 16:23

If Jesus is living in you and you have the authority of His name, if you are baptized in the Holy Ghost and you have the authority of the Holy Spirit, you can command Satan in the same way that Jesus did. Don't hesitate to take control of the situation. Don't stand idly by and watch him tear your family apart. Don't stand by and watch your world crumble. Exercise your authority, and chase the Devil from your life.

7. Prayer

Effective prayer is a powerful weapon. Jesus spent whole nights in prayer so that He could defeat every enemy and go forth victoriously to fulfill His calling in life. The important thing is to become consistent in prayer and to pray until something happens.

PUSH – Pray Until Something Happens

Don't give up. Seek and keep on seeking. Knock and keep on knocking. Ask and keep on asking. The promise of God is for all who will pay that price in prayer.

> *Ask, and it shall be given you; seek, and ye shall find; knock, and it shall be opened unto you:*
>
> Matthew 7:7

Learn to pray more than a few moments at a time. Stay before the Father's throne until the answer comes, until you have victory over the Wicked One.

8. Evangelization

Once you have learned to use these defensive weapons well, it is time to use another tactic. It is time to go on the offensive. In sports the saying is: The best defense is a good offense.

We must not just stand around warding off Satan's blows. We were destined to tear down His kingdom, to take back those who have been enslaved by his power, and to show the world that our God reigns.

We can do this by taking the battle to the enemy. Go out on his turf and use all your weapons to regain territory for our God. Face the enemy squarely and put him in his place.

> *And he said unto them, Go ye into all the world, and preach the gospel to every creature.*
> Mark 16:15

We have nothing to fear. Jesus has promised to be with us in this offensive action.

> *And, lo, I am with you alway, even unto the end of the world.* Matthew 26:66

When the disciples obeyed this command of Jesus to go forth in offensive action against the Enemy, He proved that His promise was true:

> *And they went forth, and preached every where, the Lord working with them, and confirming the word with signs following.* Mark 16:20

His promise has not changed. Go forth into the battle. You are powerful in God. Your armor is invincible in battle. Your weapons are sure. Stand up to the Evil One. Stand up and preserve what is rightfully yours. Maintain your place in God. Don't give the Devil even one inch. That is God's Word:

> *Neither give place to the devil.* Ephesians 4:27

Why should he have his way with you? Why should he harm anything that is yours? God is for you! You are powerful in Him! He has given you power over all the power of the enemy! Take your stand NOW!

> *Behold, I give unto you power to tread on serpents and scorpions, and over all the power of the enemy: and nothing shall by any means hurt you.*
> Luke 10:19

Chapter 18

Your Decision to Join the Battle

> *Choose you this day whom ye will serve; ... but as for me and my house, we will serve the Lord.*
>
> Joshua 24:15

You need God's help to overcome the Enemy, but that is no problem. God is more than eager to help you. If you have an open heart, God will move in your life. If you really want Him to set you free from the powers of Satan, He is ready to do it.

Maybe the Enemy has been deceiving you into thinking you are all right and that whatever you want to do, heaven is your home. Maybe you are one of those who says: *"I'm heaven bound, and God knows my heart."* You know your heart too, and you know that Satan's words are lies. Some things need to be put right in your life.

Maybe you are religious. You have done everything you know how to do, but are still aware — deep down in your heart — that you are not right with God. God knows all about it and wants to set you free.

Maybe you have never experienced the power of God's forgiveness through the blood of Jesus and you want to get right with Him. Don't be embarrassed by that. We all have to do it at some point in our lives. Don't be concerned with what others may think or say about it. It is between you and God. Be excited to get on His side.

Be open and honest with God. Speak to Him from your heart. He understands.

Maybe the Devil has deceived you and told you that God is not a healer. I want to tell you that healing is God's specialty.

Maybe the Deceiver told you that God no longer baptizes people in the Holy Ghost. I want to assure you that He is still doing exactly that.

Overcoming Satan and his tricks demands a decision on your part. You must get tired of his deceit. You must get tired of allowing him to ride roughshod over your life. You must say: *"Satan, I've had enough! I will not give in to you anymore. Satan, it's over with you. Don't play with me. You have no place in my life."*

That isn't so hard, is it? But no one else can make that decision for you. You must make that decision for yourself.

Aren't you tired of being tossed about by this lying thug? Do you enjoy being robbed and afflicted and cheated? Why not give God a chance with your life?

Just say: *"Satan, your lies are ended! I have discovered what you want to do in my life. And I will never again be open to you. Satan, I know now how you paint a beautiful picture and make your ways so attractive. But it's all lies. You twist the truth. I will never give in to you again.*

"I want to serve God. He really loves me. He has good things for me. I am through with you forever. I am tired of being on your altar of sacrifice. I am tired of being your slave. I am going to serve God."

If you are ready to make that commitment to God, I want to pray for you. Please pray with me right now — wherever you find yourself at this moment – and mean business with God as we pray together.

Father God,

I thank You for those who have read the pages of this book and are willing to recognize the works of Satan. The devil has indeed lied to us, but we are determined to never again collaborate with such an enemy. We will never again take sides with him. We thank You for exposing the works of darkness.

In this moment we use the authority of God vested in us and, in the name of Jesus, command that every work of Satan, every power of darkness that tries to invade the light of God's people, back off. In the name of the living God, we speak to every demon force, and we say, by the authority of

God's Word: You will not prosper in the lives of those who make a decision in this moment to commit themselves to God.

We come against sickness, disease and infirmity. We come against weakness. We come against everything that Satan has brought into our bodies in an attempt to destroy us and destroy our relationship with God. Back off! Take your hands off of the children of God. You have no right to afflict them any longer.

Lying spirits, I command you to flee in the name of Jesus.

And Father, You know that I cannot physically lay my hands upon those who are reading this book. I ask You to lay Your hands upon them. Let the power of the Holy Ghost move from the top of their heads down to the soles of their feet and make them completely free. Father, let Your glory come down upon them and drive away every evil force.

When this person finishes reading these pages, may they go forth in Your liberating truth.

Friend, Jesus is making you free. In the name of Jesus, **BE FREE** — in spirit, soul and body. The enemies of God have rejoiced over you too long. **BE FREE!** Now, the angels of heaven will rejoice over your liberation. **BE FREE!**

Every lie from Satan is now broken. **BE FREE!** In Jesus' name, **BE FREE!**

AMEN!